Geauga Lake

Copyright ©2026 by MDF Services LLC

All rights reserved. No part of this book may be used or reproduced in any manner whatsoever without written permission of the author. Published 2026

Printed in the United States of America

ISBN: 979-8-218-93444-6

Library of Congress Control Number: 2026907066

Design and layout by
Jason Price

TRAVEL / Special Interest / Amusement & Theme Parks |
HISTORY / United States / State & Local / Midwest (OH)

Published by MDF Services LLC
Irwin, Pennsylvania

Geauga Lake

ALWAYS A FUNTIME

Mike Funyak

Contents

Preface vii
Acknowledgements ix
Foreword xiii

CHAPTER 1
Giles Pond: 1817-1924 .... *1*
    Establishing Family Recreation   2
    Building a Foundation   6

CHAPTER 2
Geauga Lake Park: 1925-1968 .... *11*
    A New Era Begins   12
    The Depression Years   18
    Troubled Times   22
    A Changing Industry   28
    Creating Funtime   32

CHAPTER 3
The Funtime Era: 1969-1980 55
    The Geauga Lake Adventure   57
    All For Fun   64
    Growing Attendance   67

CHAPTER 4
Marketing Genius: 1981-1994 .... *87*
    Drench Dried Fun   88
    Funtime Guaranteed   94
    100 Years of Fun   99
    Overflowing With Fun   102

CHAPTER 5
An American Classic: 1995-1999 .... *119*
    Adding New Ingredients   123
    A New Direction   128

CHAPTER 6
Six Flags: 2000-2003.. **153**
    Four New Coasters   154
    New Guide to Fun   157
    A Wild Ride Begins   162

CHAPTER 7
Geauga Lake Forever: 2004-2007... **179**
    The Fun Is Back   181
    Two Park Fun   183
    Ongoing Challenges   187

CHAPTER 8
The Final Years: 2008-2016 .... **207**
    The Auction   208
    End of an Era   210

Appendix.. **215**
Selected Bibliography... **229**
Photo Credits... **233**
About the Author.. **237**

Preface

To write a book about an amusement park outside of the region where I was raised may seem unusual, but for those of us who grew up in the Greater Pittsburgh area, it makes perfect sense. Between 1970 and 2000, thousands of Western Pennsylvanians embarked on a one-to-two-day trip across state lines to visit Geauga Lake and Sea World in Ohio. This family trip was unmatched; only a business such as Disney could provide such a diverse level of entertainment for families. Together, the two parks attracted more than 1 million visitors each summer to Bainbridge and Aurora, Ohio.

Sea World was such a wonder for children who were fortunate enough to have visited the park. Personally, I remember meeting Pete Penguin and being filled with excitement as I watched the various marine shows. The added bonus of Geauga Lake and visiting Turtle Beach was equally memorable. I can still picture my father mowing the lawn at home, drinking water from a Geauga Lake souvenir cup that he and my mother purchased during one of the family trips. Today, that cup sits in my home - a small reminder filled with special meaning;

it's not just a souvenir cup but a symbol of my father, family, and simple joys of childhood summers.

Most of my memories from Geauga Lake consist of being at Turtle Beach, the area of the park surrounding the Big Dipper. I recall seeing the park from the Sea World stadium, riding the Skyscraper with my family, and sitting on a bench beside my mother watching the Ferris Wheel, and the massive wave pool. I can still hear The Wave siren, signaling the start of the intense waters and remember the roughness of being tossed around in them. Since that time, wave pools in the amusement industry have changed. As with anything, change occurs over time and gone are the days of overly packed wave pools with guests riding rafts. Amusement parks as I remember them from my childhood no longer exist.

When Geauga Lake became Six Flags Ohio, I remember the marketing campaign in the Pittsburgh region. People talked about visiting the park and being amazed, but my family never returned to what we still called Geauga Lake. And when Sea World was sold, I recall my siblings and I being sad because a part of our childhood was slipping away. Regretfully, I never made it back for a summer visit to Geauga Lake prior to the park's closing. At the time, it felt like an entertainment resort that would always exist. But as the saying goes, nothing lasts forever.

Geauga Lake, as it once was for over 100 years, remains only as a lasting and impactful memory. The story of how it started as a regional amusement park, developed into a modern-day amusement center, followed by an attempt to become a mega theme park, and its closure is why this book has been written. Geauga Lake as an amusement park meant so much to many families, and its legacy continues to resonate with those who were fortunate enough to experience it as we knew it best.

Acknowledgements

This book would not be possible without the support of my family. My parents David and Roseann Funyak introduced me to the world of amusement parks and were responsible for taking my siblings and me to both Geauga Lake and Sea World. I am forever thankful to have had those experiences and share them with my parents and siblings.

I also want to acknowledge and thank the following individuals:

Lee O. Bush, for sharing his memories and knowledge of Geauga Lake's long history with me as well as providing the forward for this book. Lee's extensive knowledge of the Northeast Ohio amusement park scene and encouragement to write this book were a big help in making this book possible. Lee also granted me permission to use and review the hundreds of photos Harry Peck, former Geauga Lake Publicity Director, provided to Lee and his business partners many years ago.

Charles Jacques Jr., whose amusement park books and incredible amusement park research helped inspire me to write this book. Much of the research and photos that went into this book came from Charles and Betty Jacques Amusement Park Collection.

Harry 'Henny' Henninger Jr, whose family owned Kennywood and has a long-storied history in the amusement park industry. Henny kindly shared his personal knowledge and decades of expertise, how the industry evolved, and how Kennywood and Geauga Lake remained friendly competitors for a number of years.

Sam Shurgott for sharing his personal files of Geauga Lake with me. Like myself, Sam is from the Western Pennsylvania region and visited both Geauga Lake and Sea World with his family during his youth.

Jason and Dawn Dlugonecki for sharing their personal stories of working at Geauga Lake in the 1990s as well as sharing photos for this book.

Jim Futrell who graciously provided a series of documents, particularly old advertisements from his own research files that aided in the writing of this book. Additionally, Jim provided digital scans of photos provided to him by Amusement Park Books Inc of Geauga Lake, many of which were used in this book and published for the first time.

John Kudley graciously spoke at length with me during an in-person visit to the Aurora Historical Society about Geauga Lake. His knowledge of the park and information collected by the Aurora Historical Society has been of great use in writing the early years of the park's history.

John Frato - and I had a lengthy phone conversation regarding the history of Euclid Beach Park and Cleveland area amusement parks. John strongly encouraged me to pursue writing this book about Geauga Lake to help preserve its history and significance the park had on the region and local community.

Jocko Dickey who worked at Geauga Lake for 24 years, shared great insight of the inner workings of the park's game department as well as personal memories, including those of the former Funtime Inc. ownership and management team.

Dale Van Voorhis, founder and partner of Funtime Incorporated, who purchased Geauga Lake Park in November 1968. Dale not only shared his memories and industry experience with me, he provided an ample number of detailed stories about his career in the amusement industry, including his years working at

Meyers Lake Amusement Park in Canton, Ohio, working in games, maintenance and with the office staff. I met Dale during — and by luck — at the annual IAAPA Expo in 2021 held in Orlando, Florida, through Sam Shurgott and am grateful our paths crossed.

Another thank you is extended to the Eberly Family Special Collections Library staff at Penn State University. The staff always provided excellent support and assistance during the research process.

Thank you to my editors Tim Baldwin, Dana Funyak and designer Jason Price. Jason designed an incredible cover and interior that captures the spirit of Geauga Lake.

This book is dedicated to Dale Van Voorhis.

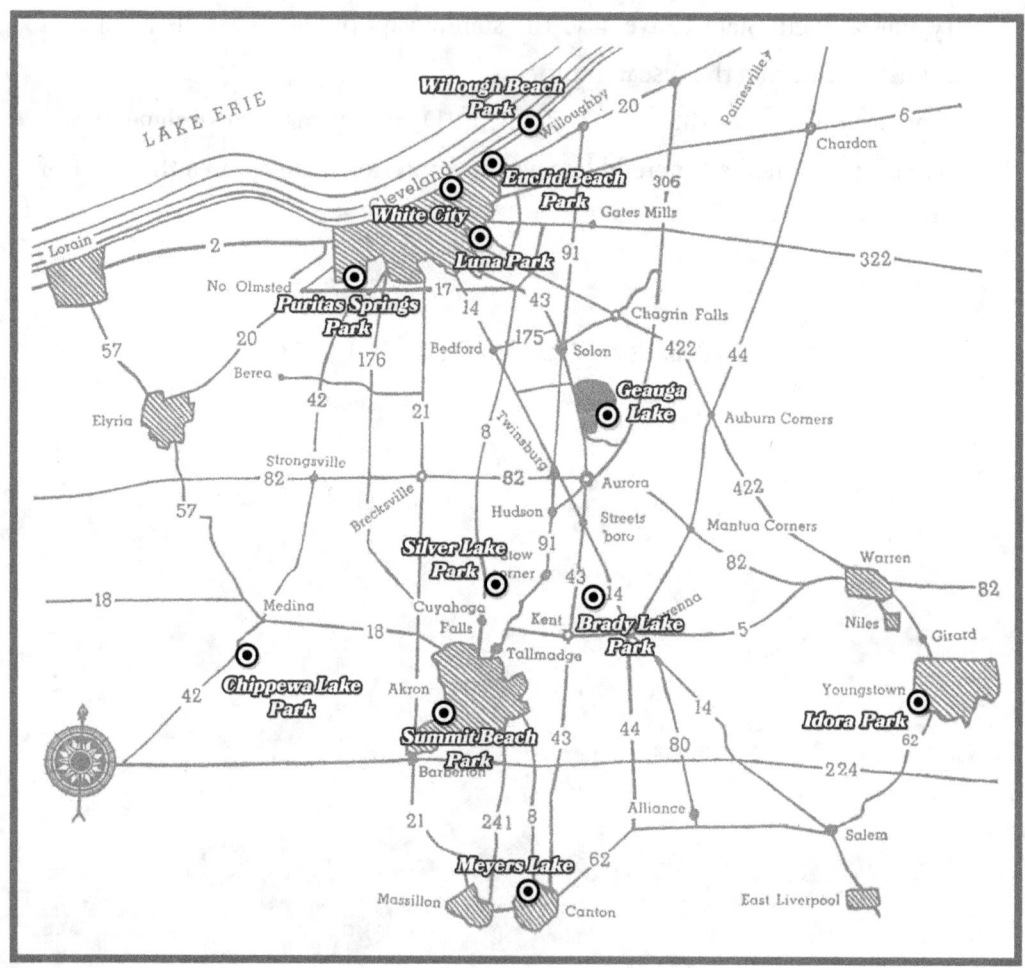

Amusement Parks of North East Ohio

Foreword

Wherever water meets land, interesting things may well occur. Rivers, lakes, an ocean, or streams; magic of sorts is a potential. Geauga Lake Park, Aurora, Ohio-southeast of Cleveland- realized some of the water/land potential. From its early days, then known as Picnic Lake — through a mixture of different amusement park blending, to now — 2025, a complete erasure of its existence is now a flotsam of commercial hodge-podge that belies what once grew from the late 1800s to the closing of the park in 2007. Anything that exists in the realm of time is permanently temporary.

For me, from somewhere in the late 1930s/early 1940s, to the present, the realm of the amusement park has, and continues to flavor my life. In those days, as a young boy, my family visited an array of parks: Cedar Point, Euclid Beach, Puritas Springs, Conneaut Lake, and of course, Geauga Lake. When Euclid Beach Park closed forever in September 1969, I felt disenfranchised. Quickly, Geauga Lake became my home park. Unlike Cedar Point and Conneaut Lake, Geauga Lake was an easy drive from my home. However, more than convenience, in the early 1970s, it had a classic charm. Nestled near the lake, there was the carousel–Illions' last machine, so they say, a Traver style Rocket Ship ride, and near to the Big Dipper roller coaster was a walkway of games and concessions along with a pier for a boat ride on Geauga Lake. It was well-worn, yet cozy, a welcome retreat. As a throw-back to the 1920s, it captured a nostalgic glow — a characterization of the golden era of the American outdoor amusement park.

As the twentieth century proceeded, new ownership developed and expanded the park. On the southeast end of the lake, Sea World was installed, making the greater Geauga Lake area a summertime destination. Some of the other older area parks: Conneaut Lake, Idora Park (Youngstown, OH) and Waldemeer (Erie, PA) carried on with minimal changes for a while. Some succumbed to declination, some continued as they were–others adapted. Geauga Lake changed continually. Funtime, Inc., Six Flags, and finally Cedar Fair all contributed to the altered landscape.

I went to Geauga Lake Park from the 1940s through to its end. The fingerprints of the 1920s lineage, and on could always be found distributed though out the park's acreage. An array of new metal coasters was added over time, and a "woody" — The Wolf Bobs — added strength to the park's appeal. In its last days Geauga Lake Park was almost a cavalcade of America's amusement park history. Read on to discover that place that was Geauga Lake Park.

— **Lee O. Bush**
AUTHOR AND AMUSEMENT PARK HISTORIAN
CLEVELAND, OHIO 2025

CHAPTER 1

Giles Pond

Déjà vu. This was the overwhelming sentiment among local residents in August 2016, when it was announced that Wildwater Kingdom, the last operating remnant of the once popular amusement park, Geauga Lake, would close at the end of the operating season.

For many, it was a painful reminder of the loss, still fresh in the memory of many residents of a similar announcement from 2007. The heartbreaking announcement that happened almost a decade earlier was that the amusement rides at Geauga Lake would cease operation. Now the region was saying goodbye to their favorite summer playground again, this time forever. The park everyone cherished would be no more; remaining only as an indelible memory of fun and special times.

At that moment, Geauga Lake joined the list of other beloved and once popular closed Northeast Ohio amusement parks: Euclid Beach Park, Meyer's Lake Amusement Park, Summit Beach Park, and Idora Park. These places, most of which were located next to lakes or bodies of water, were all once filled with the laughter of children and the sights and sounds of thrilling summer days. Those sights and sounds had now become silent and lived only in photographs, souvenirs, and memories. For generations of families, the closing of Wildwater Kingdom marked more than just the closure of a waterpark, it marked the total loss of a cherished tradition, a place synonymous with summer fun.

For well over 150 years, long before it became known as an amusement park destination, Geauga Lake had a storied past. For the duration of that time, the property that became known as Geauga Lake was always a highly trafficked area and destination. Located midway between Cleveland and Akron in Northeastern, Ohio, the property was a quiet natural retreat for local residents, one that was bound with trees and a 55-acre spring-fed lake originally known as Giles Pond or Picnic Lake.

The earliest known settler in the area that became Geauga Lake was Samuel McConoughey, who migrated from Blandford, Massachusetts, in 1806. Over the next several decades, more families settled along and near the lake's shore, first known as Picnic Lake or "The Pond." Multiple individuals and families settled on the property surrounding the lake, most notably Joel Sullivan Giles who built a log cabin as his residence in 1817. Geographically, the property was and still is divided by two counties: Geauga County to the north and Portage County to the south. Rich in natural beauty, the lake and its surrounding property gradually evolved into a gathering place for recreation and relaxation. In those earliest years, the lake and air were quiet, still untouched by the sound of thrill rides and large crowds.

Establishing Family Recreation

By the 1880s, Giles Pond was no longer a simple recreation and picnic ground, it was a destination. On a bluff at the opposite side of the lake, toward the southeast and adjacent to the Giles property, Alexander G. Kent built a famous 75-room hotel. Locals and travelers alike flocked to the resort which became known as the Kent House Hotel, later Hotel Grace, which featured popular cuisine and a modern ballroom located on the third floor. Unbeknownst to anyone at the time, this site would later be home to the Whale Stadium for Sea World of Ohio.

In addition to the Kent House, various cottages were built around the lake and made available for accommodations. During this period, attractions introduced were a roller-skating rink, photo gallery, campground, and a steam-driven carousel. Both the Kent and Giles properties and nearby businesses complemented each other with their various attractions, a concept that would draw large crowds to Geauga Lake for many years.

The Cleveland & Mahoning Railroad, chartered in 1848, began laying the first tracks through Aurora, Ohio, in 1854. A new railroad stop at Geauga Lake was a debated subject and controversy arose as to where the stop would be built. Eventually the controversy was resolved when Joel Sullivan Giles donated property for the station and a street railway system to be built. In the summertime of 1856, the glistening lake was adorned with cattails and ducks, and provided a lovely view for the railway passengers who alighted at the new stop, called Pond Station. The new Erie Railroad line ran from Cleveland through Solon, Aurora,

Kent House, 1888

Original Carousel at Geauga Lake

and later into Youngstown, Ohio. The railroad itself led to a growing workforce and general population for the area.

In 1872, Giles took advantage of the opportunity and eventually built a larger house by the new Geauga Lake Train Depot on the north side of the lake. Giles established picnic grounds, built a dance hall and brought in various forms of entertainment for local residents and train passengers seeking a day of fun. Within a few years, the resort became very popular during the summer months. The destination was known for its cleanliness and charming appeal for a single day of leisure. In 1876, a carousel first appeared and operated to the enjoyment of the general public. A short time thereafter an early roller coaster was built but later removed due to an incident resulting in injuries. While the roller coaster was not a successful attraction, Alexander Kent added a roller rink, billiard hall, and bowling alley to the delight of guests. For younger children, the resort offered pony rides which were extremely popular.

Giles Pond continued to gain popularity as an entertainment and picnic resort in large part because of its location away from the city of Cleveland. By 1880, Giles Pond was referred to as Geauga Lake. The name Geauga derives from local Native American language from those that inhabited the land in northeastern Ohio. By 1888, the addition of the first full-sized steamboat encircling the lake delighted passengers. Owned by William Bandford and Rowe Fuller, the steamboat was later purchased by the Kent Family. In addition to the steamboat, rowboats and canoes were also available on a rental basis. Boating and swimming were most popular, but it was also common for visitors to enjoy fishing on the lake.

Located on property that later became a parking lot for Sea World, now residential properties, a baseball field was built and opened on July 22 with a game between the professional baseball teams from Cleveland and Baltimore. Cleveland's National League baseball team, the Nationals, once played their home games on this very field not by choice, but by necessity. At the time, the city's strict blue laws prohibited sporting events on Sundays, enforcing a tradition of rest and religious observance. These laws, rooted in earlier centuries, restricted a range of activities on specific days, mainly Sundays. Similar to most organized sports at the time, the team found a clever workaround as games were hosted outside the city limits. For just 75 cents, fans could purchase a round-trip train ticket and admission to the game.

As crowds came and went, so did some familiar names associated with Geauga Lake. In February 1900, Alexander Kent whose name had been long tied to the area, suddenly passed away. The following month, his seven acres of land was sold to William Ryan. Along with eight more acres owned by another individual, the entire tract of property known as Kent's Grove at Geauga Lake, now only used one name. That spring, Ryan began renovating the bathhouse and pavilion and made plans to introduce free outdoor amusements. He understood the power of the lake as a draw and set out to make it a prime spot for picnics, summer outings, and growing crowds.

Despite the improvements by Ryan at the dawn of the twentieth century, the resort remained relatively quiet compared to its growing competition. Across Northeastern Ohio, recreation spots were rapidly evolving into full-fledged amusement parks. These recreation spots such as Cedar Point, Euclid Beach Park, Luna Park, Puritas Springs, Mentor Beach Playland, Idora Park, Meyers Lake Park, Brady Lake Park, Chippewa Lake, and Summit Beach Park flourished and experienced substantial growth due to the additions of mechanical amusement riding devices. The demand for amusement parks was booming with the thrills, lights, and sounds reshaping the public's idea of leisure.

Cleveland in particular was a hotbed for amusement parks. Already home to Euclid Beach Park on the eastern side of the city, a new park called White City was built in close proximity and Luna Park found its location closer to downtown. The opening of Luna Park in May 1905 became a turning point as it became Euclid Beach Park's main competitor. With more than 60,000 electric light bulbs, themed attractions, and eye-catching detailed architecture, Luna Park was a showpiece. Luna Park threatened the public parks and overall entertainment business in the area. It was developed by amusement industry pioneer Fred

Ingersoll who built, owned, and operated rides in various amusement parks, including Cedar Point. Although popular, Luna Park wasn't without controversy, which was brought on by its amenities and financial instability. The park charged for admission and sold alcohol, both of which were uncommon practices for the day. Euclid Beach, by contrast, remained free to enter and maintained a strict policy against alcohol sales.

Each season at Luna Park brought more visitors including groups that previously spent summer outings at other parks such White City, Euclid Beach Park and even Silver Lake in Akron. The other parks in and around Cleveland tried to compete by increasing entertainment and ride offerings; some failed to attract visitors, while others succeeded. The demand for amusement parks was evident. While the amusement parks in and around the city of Cleveland directly competed against each other for business, one individual who was working within the market took notice and saw opportunity in nearby Aurora.

Building a Foundation

In 1919, William "Bill" J. Kuhlman arrived at Geauga Lake and he would forever alter its future. A seasoned operator, Kuhlman saw great potential in the resort and was no stranger to the industry. He previously played pivotal roles in the opening and operation of Edgewater Park and Woodland Beach Park in Cleveland. Kuhlman was also the owner of the Broadway-Harvard bowling alleys. With an eye for opportunity and vision in mind, he established the Geauga Lake Amusement Company and went to work immediately, developing the resort for the years to come. Kuhlman envisioned transforming the existing Geauga Lake into a more modern amusement park with larger attractions, similar to the other amusement parks in Northeastern Ohio.

In an effort to attract additional visitors, the resort was rebranded. The lakeside resort was to be known and marketed as Geauga Lake Park, a name which echoed in similarity to other amusement destinations across Ohio. Kuhlman slowly began purchasing property around the lake and in 1921 purchased the property of Lola Selover. The five acres of property with its prime location along the waterfront was a key addition to his master plan. The lakefront property provided additional public access to the lake, and the Selover residence was converted into a dining hall. The construction of a brand-new dance hall on the lakeshore enabled guests to attend a daily summer dance for a mere quarter.

Like dancing, swimming was still popular with visitors, as was continued access to the lake for boating and fishing. Baseball, bowling, and tennis were other popular activities that attracted visitors. With people wanting access to the lake, Kuhlman offered property lots around the lake for sale to businesses or for the construction of cottages. Not only was Geauga Lake Park to be an amusement destination, it was to also be a community hub. The resort remained and grew in popularity under Kuhlman's watch. With the increase in popularity and visitors, Kuhlman's vision of constructing a modern-day lakeshore amusement park became more and more clear.

While Kuhlman had the management background and vision, he realized his vision would require plenty of capital and strategic partnerships. To help with this, Kuhlman attracted the attention of local businessman, attorney, and investor Harry H. Hammond who equally shared interest in transforming Geauga Lake into a premier amusement park and resort. Hammond and Kuhlman sought to gain full control of the properties surrounding the lake and succeeded.

As the pair spent time buying up properties around the lake, Kuhlman also advertised in *Billboard Magazine* seeking rides and various concession operators. In January 1925, Hammond met with the John A. Miller Company with the intention of signing an agreement for the firm to build a roller coaster at the proposed park. By the end of the month, an agreement was signed by the Northern Ohio Traction & Light company to provide electricity to the park. Beginning in February, the property began to transform into the park Kuhlman originally envisioned. The new amusement park would be located on the west shore of the lake. Work progressed rapidly to construct the new park in time for its planned opening on May 16, 1925. The half-million-dollar project was expected to make its presence felt in the local amusement park market. A total of 145 acres would be devoted for amusement purposes, with 45 acres set aside for cottages and camps, as well as a large parking area. Transportation from Cleveland and neighboring cities would be provided to Geauga Lake Park by motor bus routes in addition to the Erie Railroad. Recognizing more and more visitors were traveling by personal automobile, the addition of the bus route only proved that Kuhlman would benefit from an improved parking lot and entrance to the park. What better way to welcome guests to the renovated park but through a roller coaster, something both Luna Park and Euclid Beach featured. The new roller coaster would stand front and center signaling Geauga Lake Park as a serious player in the regional amusement park scene.

Hammond and Kuhlman certainly needed experienced help in operating the park and sought top concessionaire operators for the various games proposed for the new park. Clinton C. MacDonald, general manager of Summit Beach Park in nearby Akron, Ohio, was contacted about operating concessions at Geauga Lake Park. MacDonald was a seasoned operator who first entered the business in 1895 when he operated a popcorn and peanut concession in Hiawatha Amusement Park in Mt. Vernon, Ohio. In 1899, he worked for the Humphry Family making taffy at Euclid Beach Park and later transferred to Silver Lake Park before moving to Summit Beach Park in 1919. MacDonald's expertise proved invaluable and put Geauga Lake Park in a position for long term success. Yet competition remained strong, and Geauga Lake Park still had much to prove.

Cleveland's two premier amusement parks, Luna Park and Euclid Beach Park were now strong rivals. Facing new competition from Geauga Lake Park was not considered a threat. Both Luna Park and Euclid Beach had a strong reputation and share of the local market, as did Summit Beach Park in Akron. Eventually, the Humphrey Family of Euclid Beach Park emerged as the leader of all Cleveland and Northeast Ohio amusement parks. The Humphrey Family, owners of Euclid Beach Park, invested heavily in new rides, including the expansion of Kiddieland and new roller coasters through 1930. This was a goal for the new Geauga Lake Park, but it would take years until the park could heavily invest into rides to the level of Euclid Beach Park. Geauga Lake would need time to grow in popularity but Kuhlman and Hammond laid the foundation for which decades of fun would commence.

Pony rides were a popular early attraction

4th OF JULY AT GEAUGA LAKE.

If you are looking for a pleasant place to spend the 4th, come to Geauga.
FINE ATTRACTIONS, GOOD MUSIC.
GREAT SKATING RACE
For Five Mile Championship of Ohio, between John Bell, of Cleveland, and Geo. Reed, of Alliance.
Excursion rates, and ALL trains stop on the 3d, 4th and 5th.
Independence Ball at Kent House evening of July 3.

HOTEL GRACE
GEAUGA LAKE.
Now open; 20 miles from Cleveland, on Erie Ry.; boating, bathing, fishing, etc.; first-class hotel, without intoxicants; write for rates by day or week.

GEAUGA LAKE PARK
Thursday, June 26, 1924
County Night for the Families and Friends of Ravenna, Mantua, Aurora, Hiram, Kent and Garrettsville
25c Dancing from 8 to 12 o'clock
Come Early   Bring a Basket Lunch
BATHING   BOATING   TENNIS   BASEBALL
DANCING EVERY NIGHT
SOCIAL DANCING EVERY MONDAY & FRIDAY NIGHTS
Other dates for the same folks July 17th, Aug. 14th & 23rd

Opening Tonight
Geauga Lake
Dancing Pavilion

Dancing Every Evening and Sunday Afternoon and Evening

New Pavilion just completed at the edge of the lake. Hamley's union vocal orchestra. Special nights can be arranged for clubs and Social Dances.

Good paved road—19 miles from Public Square. Street cars to 131st and Corlett, or to Randall, Center road. Bus line from 131st and Corlett and 105th and Euclid. Bus line also from Ravenna, Chagrin Falls and Kent.

"We Own the Lake"   The Geauga Lake Amusement Co.
Wm. J. Kuhlman, Mgr.

CHAPTER 2

Geauga Lake Park

Located approximately 25 miles southeast of Cleveland and 30 miles north of Akron on State Route 43, Geauga Lake Park became an amusement park where more and more people of northeastern Ohio flocked to visit. The park was ready to introduce new attractions, most notably a massive 3,200-foot roller coaster costing $50,000 (just shy of $1 million in 2025, a century later). Designed and built by the country's leading roller coaster designer and ride broker, the John Miller Company, the new lakeside ride quickly became an icon for the park.

Before guests could experience the thrill of riding the new lakeside roller coaster, they had to travel to the park. The roadways to Geauga Lake had drastically improved in the years since Kuhlman's arrival as more visitors began arriving at the park without the need of the local street car and railroads. Improved roadways to Aurora were necessary if the park would ever see consistent revenue and one that allowed for future growth.

Though not enough work had yet been accomplished to improve the indirect route of travel from Cleveland, it was a step in the right direction. On Sundays, train services were arranged to bring visitors to the park, and later, regular bus route services were introduced. The location of the park worked to its benefit as new owners of automobiles looked to travel with family away from the busy cities and into the country. The park's rural location became a major asset as the automobile became the preferred method of transportation.

To accommodate this shift, the park advertised new parking spaces that could hold between 5,000-7,000 cars. As the automobile slowly became the primary means of transportation, more and more people began purchasing property away from the city forming suburbs. It proved pivotal that the road ways accommodate the increase in motorists and area residents. The area around Geauga Lake was about to experience a spike in population. Geauga Lake Park occupied a total of 300 acres of land at the time with 75 acres devoted to free parking. The parking area was monitored by uniformed attendants and was gated with a single entrance to promote safety. This controlled access in and out of the resort.

A New Era Begins

With the installation of a perimeter fence, the park needed a formal entrance due to the recent updates. Purposely designed to impress guests, the new main entrance was a marvel, leading guests under and through the structure of the Sky Rocket roller coaster.

Advertised as 3,200 feet long, the ride was actually only 2,800 feet and stood 65 feet tall. It was an out-and-back-style roller coaster with typical design elements such as a double dip. The John Miller Company not only built the roller coaster but brokered other attractions added to the park in 1925 such as The Dodgem, Circle Swing, Carousel and Skee-Ball alleys for the new Penny Arcade. Other amusements included the Whip, Hey Dey, an auto speedway, and a Miniature Train. The miniature train purchased from Dayton Fun House and Riding Device Manufacturing Company was bought to provide a short line railroad connecting the Erie Railroad with the park. A new shooting gallery, marketed as the largest in the country, added to the growing list of amusements. A new era of fun had certainly arrived!

Sky Rocket Construction

Prior to opening for the 1925 season, many projects needed completion. One ongoing project was the construction of a water tower, which required drillers to dig over 100 feet before hitting water. The pump for the water was run all day to acquire an adequate supply of water for the park. The new Sky Rocket roller coaster successfully took its first test run, and the Carousel building was completed with a new Wurlitzer band organ installed. Restrooms were still in the process of being completed when the park opened, with the women's restroom being the lone exception. Discussions about administering admission fees to rides were debated; pay as you enter or pay as you leave. Ultimately pay as you enter was decided upon for the amusement rides.

With the numerous additions and ongoing projects, the park's formal opening did not occur until Saturday, June 20, 1925. When the new Geauga Lake Park did open, it was an instant success with park goers. The multi-year expansion capital improvement plan established a theme that continued into the years ahead. Picnic tables were added to accommodate 12,000 picnickers and a covered pavilion on the lake shore had a seating capacity of 4,000. The grounds were naturally spacious, and while the athletic sports such as the baseball field and tennis courts remained, swimming in the lake was no longer permitted. Instead, the ownership

The Carousel Building shown under construction was designed by John A. Miller.

group decided to construct a new swimming pool and have 100 row boats available for rent on the lake.

The new pool was not planned to launch for the 1925 summer months, but was anticipated to build excitement for the following summer and prove to guests that ownership was committed to turning Geauga Lake Park into the area's premier amusement park. Plans for the swimming pool began in early May with a steam shovel excavating the site. Restrictions for the pool's placement had to be lifted. The pool and bath house couldn't be more than 10 feet above grade due to a proposed road that followed the lake from the Erie Railroad Depot. When finished, the new swimming pool was 350 feet long by 100 feet wide. Excitement grew as construction was completed in August, and the pool opened in September. However, with it being so late in the season, Hammond delayed the "official grand opening" until the following season.

When the park opened for the season in April 1926, it advertised the swimming pool as its new attraction, which would open on Memorial Day. The park was open Saturdays and Sundays through May and afterwards was open daily through Labor Day. The pool, which operated from 9:30 a.m. to 10 p.m., was illuminated at night with the rest of the park. It featured diving boards and a sand beach. To enter the pool area, guests had to pay a 10-cent admission fee. The depth of the water varied from one end to the other, and the deepest section of the pool was 14 feet. In what was common practice for the era, the pool was drained and cleaned each evening at closing. A detailed and long process, the park was committed to providing a clean and safe environment for everyone. Since Euclid Beach Park had earned a reputation as an exceptionally clean park, the precedent had been set for similar businesses in close proximity. The idea of promoting and maintaining a clean, presentable park was made a priority.

On July 18, 1926, Olympic swimmer Johnny Weissmuler, later known for his acting career, set a new world record for the 220-yard freestyle in the Geauga Lake Park swimming pool. Weissmuler competed in the 1924 and 1928 Summer Olympics on the United States men's swimming and water polo teams. He was also known for having one of the best competitive swimming records for his time. He brought national attention to Geauga Lake Park with his record-breaking swim.

The entrance to Geauga Lake Park. The original design included an on-site police and fire station, along with protective safety barriers.

That same year, improvements continued elsewhere in the park, including new locker rooms and showers at the baseball field. The park even established its own baseball team. President Hammond remained focused on promoting Geauga Lake Park as a family park in order to attract the much-needed crowds to sustain steady business. He even purchased advertising space in the *Cleveland Plain Dealer* and the *Cleveland Press*. Hammond took an active part in keeping families at the top of the park's mission and personally held the motto of "Good, clean amusement." Hammond was quoted and emphasized in the July 5, 1927 edition of the *Cleveland Plain Dealer*:

> *"Everything that we have built and everything that we are building for the future must be dignified and clean. We feel the public want clean amusement. We particularly cater to picnics, and the indications are that more than 150 organizations will have held their picnics at Geauga Lake before the season is over. We are constantly on the lookout for new attractions. The transportation problem has been solved through regular Sunday and holiday service via the Erie Railroad as well as the special picnic service by that road."*

Amusement rides and recreation sports were not the only attractions at the park. Guests were encouraged to drive to the park for a steak or chicken dinner at the J.H. Allendorf, the park's primary dining hall, and remain afterward for dances featuring the best of the latest orchestras. Owner-operator J.H. Allendorf was

J.H. Allendorf, the parks dining hall

invited to operate a restaurant at the new park in large part because his Allendorf Restaurant located in Cleveland was Hammond's favorite place to dine and conduct business meetings. The community of Geauga Lake was established in 1927 as a village with a 265-to-68 "in favor" vote. The reason for establishing the village was to reduce taxes and to improve conditions for the park so it could continue to invest in the future. The hope was to remove the blue laws which restricted dances on Sunday. Hammond recognized dances were a major draw for the park and hoped his conversations with Portage County Sheriff James and Judge Robison would help facilitate dancing to occur on Sundays. Even with the help of area businessmen, the efforts were unsuccessful. Elsewhere in the local area, the Bainbridge Park racetrack opened in 1927 on property adjacent to Geauga Lake Park. Built by John King and Homer Kline, the one-mile race track entertained fans until its closure in 1956. The track hosted horse races and auto races, including NASCAR sanctioned events.

To increase ridership to the area, the Erie Railroad offered service every Sunday and holiday to the park in 1927. Further improvements to the roads leading to the park continued into 1928 with the parking lot to accommodate 25,000 cars. The expanded parking area also featured an aviation field that was used for airplane rides and entertainment. The park began attracting crowds, not just for the new amusements but also to see and listen to noted speakers. During a picnic in 1928, William Green, president of the American Federation of Labor, gave a notable speech to an estimated 45,000 guests about defending "the rights of labor in the machine age."

By this time, the park was competing directly with Euclid Beach Park, Luna Park, and Cedar Point. Other parks such as Chippewa Lake, Brady Lake, Summit Beach, and Puritas Springs Park also advertised in the local newspapers. The new park attracted a lot of attention from the local community and even from other nearby amusement parks. People were eager to see the new Geauga Lake Park. Even Dudley Humphrey of nearby Euclid Beach Park attended one of the park's opening days in the 1920s. What these other Northeastern Ohio amusement parks had as a major advantage over Geauga Lake was that they still benefited from better transportation. Both Euclid Beach and Luna Park were on Cleveland's trolley lines while Kuhlman and Hammond had to rely on buses. It was a work in progress, but by 1929 Kuhlman expected to have the transportation issue solved. In May 1929, Kuhlman entered into an agreement with Cleveland Street Railway Company to have buses offer round trips with a ticket good for a ride or a dance.

Another advantage Luna Park had over Geauga Lake was the selling of alcohol inside the park. Geauga Lake elected not to sell alcoholic drinks, as businesses on the neighboring property and roads to and from the park served alcohol. By the end of 1928, Cleveland's Luna Park closed as the selling of alcoholic drinks was halted during Prohibition catapulting the park into debt from lost revenue and declining attendance. The park was shuttered for two years and eventually sold at a sheriff's sale. Interestingly, John Gooding of nearby Puritas Springs Park purchased Luna Park's carousel. Once Luna Park was razed, residential properties appeared on the site.

The Depression Years

By the end of the decade, Geauga Lake Park utilized a variety of marketing slogans such as "The Park that is better and the best, Different than the rest" and "A Park for all the family." In 1929, the park advertised itself as "The Spot for Your Weekend Vacation," and in the early 1930s, "The Cleanest Park in Ohio." Unfortunately, the park's success that occurred from the mid-to-late 1920s would not last. As the country dealt with the economic impact of the Great Depression, businesses only spent money in order to survive. However, the Great Depression did not halt Kuhlman's plans of installing the Tumble Bug in 1930.

Many families spent significantly less money during the Great Depression because of little or total loss of income. Money that might have been used on entertainment was now spent to support the livelihood of families. Most amusement parks added few attractions and relied on dancing to attract crowds during the Great Depression. Orchestras that performed at Geauga Lake during this decade included Kay Kayster's Orchestra, Carlone's Orchestra, Lou Piatt's Playboys, George Williams and his Orchestra, and Allen Smith and his Orchestra. In the

1920s, orchestras were paid $1,000 for a week's worth of performances, but in the 1930s, orchestras traveled more frequently and only received $600 a week.

In 1931, Geauga Lake Park and Conneaut Lake Park in Pennsylvania served as training camps for Willie Stribling, the Pride of Georgia, contender for the World's Heavy Weight Championship held by Max Schmeling. When the two boxers held their match on July 3, it was the first event held in Cleveland Stadium with Schmeling retaining the title. The following year a new highway from Cuyahoga County to the Geauga Lake Park opened, further increasing access to the park. Park management made sure to have enough parking guards on South Miles Roads to prevent traffic congestion. The new roadway augmented guest patronage, and when Prohibition ended in 1933, the opening of a large Beer Garden offered a new revenue stream for the park. The new Beer Garden was advertised as the largest beer garden in the Midwest, although the park was not really located in the Midwest. State Senator Joseph N. Ackerman, author of the Ohio beer law, was on hand at the formal opening of the Beer Garden. Ackerman said of the day:

> *"Places like this are the first indication of a return to sanity and the marking of the end of fanaticism and idiocy under prohibition."*

The new Beer Garden, completed in only 24 days, sold beer for 20 cents, enabling Kuhlman to attract additional group businesses. By 1934, Geauga Lake Park began to claim it attracted over a million guests per year. That number was more than likely overestimated. Typical of the times, parks boasted they had record attendance. That season marked Kuhlman's 15th year as Geauga Lake's vice president and general manager and while the Great Depression was hampering the economy, Kuhlman, along with other park owners and operators, knew entertainment had the potential to attract crowds and bring people together. The general public had little money to spend, and park owners knew if they wanted to remain afloat, they needed to attract crowds, and no better option existed but to host music and entertainment. This was the era of the Big Bands, and guests commonly visited the park to dance and move to the sights and sounds of the day's popular entertainers.

Nightly operatic presentations became a popular feature during the summer of 1934. Music entertainers who performed at Geauga Lake included Guy Lombardo, trumpeter, Henry Busse, along with Shep Fields and His Rippling Rhythm Orchestra. Fans of Appalachian-style folk music, a precursor of country music, were equally excited to hear the Corn Creek Girls Band and Homer "Slim" Miller at the park. The new Beer Garden not only faced the lake, it featured an entertainment stage. On various nights, fireworks were shot out over the lake to the delight of park guests. In 1938, Mardi Gras firework festivals, a popular party trend at amusement parks at the time, featured displays of the sinking of the Lusitania and Commodore Perry's battle of Lake Erie.

With funds generated from the Beer Garden, the park introduced a beautiful five-row Marcus Illions Carousel featuring 64 hand-carved horses. Built and hand-carved in 1926, the ride was considered one of the most valuable carousels in the world. Originally built for the Sesqui-Centennial Celebration held in Philadelphia in 1927, the Carousel moved to Birmingham, Alabama. When the ride arrived at Geauga Lake on trucks, it was dismantled and damaged. Marcus Illions completed work on the band organ façade with painting and leafing. Elmer Tucek, one of the park's maintenance workers, recalled Illions accompanied by two of his sons spending the entire pre-season repairing and restoring the ride to mint condition. Tucek helped in the restoration process and remembered Illions, a lover of horses, had a disdain for animals other than horses on carousels. Costing an estimated $35,000, the ride was placed in the existing carousel pavilion located overlooking the lake in what was considered the heart of the park on the main midway.

The Illions Carousel was considered a premium brand and was one of only a few five-row carousels manufactured in Marcus C. Illions factory in Coney Island, New York. In addition to the 64 all-jumping horses, the ride featured 54 reflecting mirrors on the rounding boards. The ride remained one of Geauga Lake's most popular and historic attractions for the duration of the park's tenure as an amusement park. After adding the new carousel, the park attempted to sell the older Philadelphia Toboggan Carousel, but was unable to find a buyer. The ride remained, but was covered with a canvas and only used for large group outings until it was eventually sold.

The park's growing success was not just the work of Hammond and Kuhlman, but additional tenured employees, who began working at the park in the early 1920s. Joe Wilt started at Geauga Lake working at the ballroom and rose in the ranks to become park superintendent. Wilt's wife, Irene, also worked at the ballroom beginning in 1923, where the couple met and fell in love. In addition to Joe, his brother Ed worked at the park in maintenance, and he too met his wife who worked at the Garden Theater in the park.

Orville Slater and the Wilts became known as "the three," meaning they all started working at the park's ballroom. Similar to Joe Wilt, Slater also met his wife while working at the park. Joe Becka, another long-term tenured employee, was the arcade manager. Becka previously owned and operated the bus line that transported patrons to the ballroom from 1921 to 1924. Other long-term employees included roller coaster operator Bill Fisher, games concessionaire J.J. McCarthy, boatman Clark Gable, swimming pool manager Red Weisenbach, Chief of Police Charley Linert, and ride operator Charles Schryer.

In 1938, Bill Kuhlman sold ownership of the park to his nephews, Charles and Harvey Schryer. At the time, Viola Schryer, wife to Harvey, worked as Kuhlman's personal secretary. Viola's mother was interestingly a long-time employee at the park, working the novelty stand inside the main entrance, which led Viola to work at the park and meet Charles. Kuhlman eventually saw Viola and other members of the Schryer Family as the next generation of leaders for the park. Beginning the following year, the Schryer brothers began purchasing the park's land, parcel by parcel.

In June 1939, Geauga Lake celebrated both the park's 15th anniversary and the 20th anniversary of the ballroom. Park officials were excited to open the week with the annual Cleveland Retail Meat Dealers Association picnic and finish the week with an outing by the Quaker State Clubs. By the end of the decade, the park had grown exponentially in spite of the Great Depression. Geauga Lake Park and its property, which had previously attracted people to its natural lake, was now attracting thousands of visitors each summer for amusements and a variety of entertainment.

Minor improvements were made to the park, such as the Circle Swing receiving new silver rocket ships. The silver rocket ship concept was conceived, designed, and installed by the Humphrey Family at nearby Euclid Beach Park on their Circle Swing. The concept of adding new futuristic, space-oriented ride vehicles was not common during that era, but proved to be an extremely popular idea. This idea of the Humphrey's encouraged the R.E. Chambers Company of Beaver Falls, Pennsylvania, successor of the original manufacturer of the Circle Swing, Traver Engineering, to develop and market their own version of silver rocket ships to parks with older circle swings. Geauga Lake was not the only nearby park to make this investment as Meyers Lake in Canton and Idora Park in Youngstown followed suit. This proved cost effective and helped reimagine an existing ride by making it a new experience. The idea that what is old was new again proved successful.

Troubled Times

After the turn of the 20th century, the United States contained almost 2,000 amusement parks, but by the end of the Great Depression, that number shrunk to roughly 500. Because public dances attracted crowds, Bill Kuhlman invested in a new ballroom for 1941. The inaugural dance featured Gill Crest and his Orchestra. The Aurora Volunteer Fireman also prepared 75 door prizes to be awarded with proceeds going toward the fire fighters benefit fund.

The following season, 1942, saw the park open on May 16. The ongoing war in Europe and attack on Pearl Harbor in December 1941 escalated world tensions and forced many young workers to join the armed services. The park committed to its plans for 1943, which included unveiling two new rides: the Fly-O-Plane and a dark ride first known as the Blackout. The new rides brought the park ride lineup to 18 and a total of 55 midway attractions. Additionally, management expected large picnics to attract 50,000 guests and were optimistic in attracting crowds, it was largely known that the workforce had shrunk and many working

The Fly-O-Plane featured 8-themed vehicles with two guest controlled steering wheels, which activated the vehicles rotation.

aged individuals began contributing to the war efforts. Companies of all sizes altered their operations to manufacture materials for the war. The United States' involvement in World War II was ramping up, and the park pushed forward in its goal to provide family entertainment.

The season's success was hampered by a late August tornado that caused an estimated $50,000-$60,000 in damages. Described as "a baby cyclone," a next-day check of the park uncovered damage to the ballroom and an entire section of the Sky Rocket structure was knocked over, crushing the bingo building and leaving the Penny Arcade roof less. About 100 individuals escaped injury because parts of the Sky Rocket structure fell on the rear of the buildings. The ballfields' grandstands were flattened, a total of 50 trees were knocked over or branches damaged, and six guests were injured. An estimated 15 to 20 acres of trees on one side of the lake were leveled. Kuhlman was not pleased with the damage, but certainly relieved that park officials had taken precautions by closing 30 minutes before most of the damage occurred from the storm. Witnesses who saw the funnel cloud approaching the park said that if the tornado had altered course, hundreds of individuals inside the arcade may have been injured as the funnel cloud was an estimated 100 yards from the building.

The park opened the following year with a rebuilt midway, Sky Rocket, and new Ferris Wheel. Putting additional focus on successful weekend operations and picnic days, Geauga Lake Park enjoyed a strong 1943 season. The park remained closed on weekdays and day group picnics were not scheduled. War-worker outings were successful events for the park on weekends as well as during the week. The Jack and Heintz Company, a nationally known war plant, held a picnic at Geauga Lake Park on July 5. This company outing brought more than 50,000 visitors and provided the park with its best single day in park history. Kuhlman remarked in a September 11 edition of *Billboard Magazine* that while some parks and resorts of the Greater Cleveland area did not open in 1943, Geauga Lake Park remained open every Sunday in September and provided war-worker families with needed recreation.

In the early 1940s, George P. Smith Jr., former salesman and general manager of Philadelphia Toboggan Company (PTC), joined the Geauga Lake Park staff. One of his first tasks was to sell some of the park's older rides, such as the carousel, the Spillman Engineering Hey-Day, and a #5 Eli-Bridge Ferris Wheel. During Smith's time at the park, B.A. Schiff supplied the park with 80 rowboats for the lake. The lake was also stocked with Bluegill fish and bass. Smith was a great addition to the team at Geauga Lake Park because of his industry knowledge and experience. However his tenure was cut short when he died unexpectedly of a heart attack. Then, in late July 1944, Bill Kuhlman tragically lost his life in an automobile accident at the age of 60 in Maples Height, Ohio. The local community was shocked and overcome by grief. Kuhlman was a beloved figure by the local community and his loyal employees. At the time of his passing, Kuhlman's remaining ownership was sold to local attorney Carl Adrion and William Terrel. Charles Schryer was named park president and general manager and his brother Harvey became secretary-treasurer. Following the end of World War II, Viola Schryer's sister, Genevieve Solinsky and her husband Paul joined the park's management team. Genevieve managed one of the park's food outlets and novelty stores while her husband, Paul, took over management of the ballroom. The park truly remained a family business and operation.

In 1946, the park operated on a six-days-a-week schedule. 1946 was the first season since before the war that the park operated regularly during the week.

About $500,000 was spent on park projects by the time the park opened on May 5. The Sky Rocket roller coaster was rebuilt with a new lift hill, transfer track, and brakes. The rebuilding of the Sky Rocket was delayed until 1946 for two reasons: restrictions of materials in 1942 and 1943 and Kuhlman's untimely passing. Herbert Schmeck and the Philadelphia Toboggan Company who also completed work on the roller coasters at Euclid Beach were contracted to rebuild the Sky Rocket. The ride modifications and new modernized loading station were also designed and supervised by Herbert Schmeck. The park wished to have a redesigned coaster station and elected to rename the roller coaster as the Clipper. As the Schyrer brothers looked to modernize the look of the park's buildings in a post-World War II society, inspiration for new park architecture came from Coney Island in Cincinnati, Ohio. Other money was spent on a new building to feature a Cuddle Up ride and new popcorn and frozen custard machines.

The following year saw the park hit a rough patch. A fire destroyed the bathhouse early in the season, though a new and modern one quickly replaced the ruined one. Luckily, both the Clipper and Fun House were spared from the flames. Later in the season, a guest claimed to have suffered paralysis resulting from an injury sustained on the Dodgem which resulted in a $75,000 lawsuit. Another fire, five years later damaged the bowling alley, theater and ballroom

The charred remains of the ballroom after the 1952 fire

which hosted roller skating. The ballroom, which was converted into a roller rink for year-round revenue, was one of the largest roller skating rinks in Northeastern Ohio. Also lost in the fire was the band organ for the Carousel. While park management was reluctant to estimate damage, Park Attorney Carl Adrion said:

> "Loss will certainly be in excess of $150,000. To replace these buildings might cost as much as $500,000."

The fire damage was a massive blow to the Geauga Lake's featured attractions. Local news reports of the flames being seen from miles away led to speculation about the park's future. The Clipper roller coaster was spared from flames by the Aurora Township Fire Department, but key attractions were lost and the conflict on the Korean peninsula made purchasing steel virtually impossible. Since steel was unable to be purchased, a decision was made to dismantle a gambling hall that stood on the park's property across the lake. The ballroom had been a revenue-generating machine that proved vital to the park's future so the decision to dismantle the gambling hall was made with little to no hesitation. After all, most of the park property across the lake remained undeveloped in regard to the actual amusement park. A new ballroom was constructed with steel beams from the gambling hall and built behind the turnaround of the Clipper, next to Aurora Road. This cost-effective move was a great business decision and the new ballroom opened later in the season.

With the end of World War II and following the trend of other amusement parks, Geauga Lake Park began installing additional children rides to the park to meet the demand of the Baby Boom. Military men returning home from the war were quick to start families, and, all of a sudden, a huge demand existed to entertain young families and children. The park continued its 6-day weekly operations and remained closed on Monday, with Decoration Day and Labor Day being the exception. Additions included new roller coaster cars from the National Amusement Device Company and cars for the Loop-O-Plane. For the families and children, The Little Dipper, a junior roller coaster designed and built by National Amusement Device (NAD) opened and the following year came the installation of more rides that would remain favorites for the foreseeable future; the Rock-O-Plane, the Midge-O-Racer, and Bulgy the Whale.

During this era, Geauga Lake lagged behind its nearby competitors, Euclid Beach and Puritas Springs, in terms of cleanliness and overall reputation. While both of those parks were known for being exceptionally clean and considered top-tier destinations, Geauga Lake was often viewed as a second-tier facility. Still, like many regional amusement parks at the time, it remained a popular local attraction. However, as the years went on, a lack of adaptability began to affect many amusement parks in the post–World War II era, including Geauga Lake.

That began to change in 1954, when an unexpected and dramatic event sparked a shift. One night, a security guard on duty heard suspicious noises coming from the lake. Moments later, four armed men attempted to rob the park's main office and the on-site residence of Genevieve Solinsky and her family. Genevieve lived at the park with her husband, Paul; her sister, Viola; and Viola's husband, Charles Schryer. The robbers had arrived by rowboat, carrying firearms and containers of gasoline. Their target was a safe inside the house, believed to contain around $20,000 in company funds. It was suspected the burglars had prior knowledge that the money was stored there. Although the night guard managed to disrupt the robbery, he was shot in the leg and hip during the confrontation. Fortunately,

Park residence, the Schryer House

the robbery was ultimately unsuccessful. Deeply shaken by the incident, the Solinsky family moved out of the house just three days late. This decision marked a turning point in the park's awareness of its vulnerabilities and the need to adapt.

A Changing Industry

Times were changing and similar to Geauga Lake, other nearby parks such as Cedar Point, Chippewa Lake Park, Meyers Lake Amusement Park, Idora Park, Waldameer Park and Conneaut Lake Park proved they could survive. Most of these facilities featured large bodies of water next to the parks, which allowed for fishing, boating, and swimming. The economic downturn of 1955 and 1956 forced Geauga Lake Park management to reduce the price of ride tickets to five cents every Friday in July and August. In the 1950s, there was a notion that renaming existing attractions at amusement parks was the "in" trend. A perfect example of this was when the Schryer's renamed the Whip to The Snap.

With the opening of Disneyland in Anaheim, California, in 1955, park owners and operators were forced to change their ways and methods in how they operated their parks. While some industry executives were skeptical of Walt Disney's vision for an amusement park with themes to his characters, Disneyland quickly became a force within the amusement industry and coerced park owners to beef up their business practices. The opening of Disneyland dislodged the outlook of the amusement industry and what the future held, especially when it came to capital dollars spent and future expenditures. The addition of new rides at parks was growing in popularity and became the main driver for the increase in daily and overall season attendance. The annual investment of purchasing and installing new rides became a financial burden for some parks, so much so that they simply went out of the business. Other park owners could not establish plans quickly enough, as a lot of swift changes were taking the industry by storm.

Disneyland was not the only theme park in the industry that opened during the 1950s. A number of other themed amusement parks opened across the country along with numerous kiddie parks featuring only children's attractions. Because of these new trends, a lot of amusement park owners were unable to modernize or resisted modernizing with the times. Even dances and music entertainment began to lose popularity. Due to aging equipment and infrastructure, some parks simply closed and sold out because their property value was more valuable than the actual amusement park business. One particular park purchased for redevelopment was Cedar Point. Cedar Point had fallen so far behind the times that many Clevelanders stopped visiting. Being that Cedar Point had lost its charm and was more difficult to travel to from Cleveland, Geauga Lake and other parks in Northeast Ohio benefitted.

Purchased in the late 1950s by George Roose of Toledo, Ohio, and Emilie Legros of Cleveland, Ohio, Cedar Point was purchased with the intent to close and develop the land into a marina and residential property. This plan was blocked by the local government, leading Roose and Legros to spend $16 million over a number of years to redevelop Cedar Point into a premier amusement park. A consulting firm from Los Angeles, California, was hired to develop a five-year plan for the facility with most of the aging rides and buildings removed. Cedar Point was previously offered to other amusement park owners and operators, but many declined to even consider taking over the facility. Owning and operating multiple amusement parks was not a common practice of the day, and Cedar Point was in rough condition. Even the owners of Kennywood Park near Pittsburgh, Pennsylvania, declined to purchase the resort due to its less-than-ideal location and the overall condition of the facility. The revitalization of Cedar Point turned into one of the great success stories in the history of the amusement park industry. Had Cedar Point closed, the future and story of the Northeastern Ohio amusement park scene would be totally different.

The revitalization of Cedar Point changed the future of other amusement parks in Ohio, which included Euclid Beach Park, Meyers Lake Amusement Park, Summit Beach Park, Idora Park, and Chippewa Lake Park. These older traditional family amusement parks were forced to be cleaner, rebuild existing buildings to accommodate growth, and expand attraction offerings. Amusement parks were pressured to enact new business models, and parks everywhere had to change their ways. While some of the previously mentioned parks elevated their standards, Euclid Beach Park maintained the status quo. In 1958, after years of declining attendance, the Gooding Family, owners of Puritas Springs Park, closed the park and sold the property to residential developers. Additionally, Summit Beach Park, once known as Akron's Million Dollar Playground, closed as well. This began the gradual shrinkage of the Northeast Ohio amusement park scene. The theme park mentality impacted every amusement park operator.

As society and culture in the United States shifted in the late 1950s, people expected the 1960s to host even more changes. Coney Island in Cincinnati, Ohio, the most popular and attended amusement park in the state, now had a new competitor. Had Cedar Point closed, it would not have provided the amusement industry at large with the business model most parks needed to move the industry forward. Additionally, the revitalization of Cedar Point and the need to hire young business professionals would have had a negative impact on the future of Geauga Lake Park, especially for those who envisioned owning their own amusement park.

Charles and Harvey Schryer continued to reinvest in Geauga Lake Park in the late 1950s and into the 1960s. The brothers worked diligently to pay off their debt and add new rides to support the growing business. Charles Schryer not only spent his time as president of Geauga Lake Park, but he also worked as the park's picnic manager to attract more than 100 group picnics each season and designed multiple buildings at the park. The park did not charge general admission, but the estimated average seasonal attendance was around 1 million visitors a year. Geauga Lake Park provided summer seasonal jobs for 130 individuals and operated all rides and most of its food operations. Concessionaires continued to operate the games, arcade, shooting gallery, and some food stands. Eight full-time employees, including the Schryer brothers, worked year-round. Genevieve Solinsky and her sister Viola Schryer spent much of the offseason polishing and cleaning the carousel and its horses.

Embracing the new generation of modern, nontraditional rides, Park President Charles Schryer invested in a Wild Mouse roller coaster for 1958. It was the park's first nontraditional roller coaster in that it was a steel roller coaster featuring sharp runs and steep drops. What made this ride different was that it could be dismantled and moved easily. Portable rides began to appear in many amusement parks at this time as the rides did not require the preparation of that of a permanent ride. If a portable ride was deemed unpopular, it could be easily

removed and replaced by another attraction. If a park owner wished to move it elsewhere in the park to accommodate another new attraction, the portable ride could be moved. The introduction of portable rides to permanent or fixed parks was a smart investment allowing park owners to be creative with midway space and expansion projects. The concept of relocating rides throughout a park allowed parks to spread out crowds while introducing something new.

The following year in September 1959, local Cleveland radio station WHK held a free appreciation night at Geauga Lake Park. The event featured a rock-and-roll show with popular entertainers such as Bobby Rydell and Freddy Cannon. Freddy Cannon would soon have a massive hit with his 1962 song, Palisades Park, which was based on a visit to the then popular New Jersey amusement park. The event at Geauga Lake Park brought an estimated 25,000 guests and a special police escort was required to help the entertainers into the park. With rock and roll becoming popular, music acts started to have a resurgence in popularity at amusement parks and roller skating fell out of popularity. In 1962, the park closed its Roller Rink which included a bowling alley and large bar. The building was closed and the roller skates were placed in storage. As tastes changed, amusement park owners had to decide: keep everything from the past or keep some of the past and innovate to ensure solvency with the general public. As Geauga Lake entered the 1960s, it was clear, keeping everything from the past was not going to keep the park relevant.

The 1960s saw fewer additions to Geauga Lake Park as the Schryer brothers contemplated selling their park and retiring, similar to other local competitors. A lack of sound decision-making for the future and uncertainty of the industry may have led the Schryer brothers to this conclusion. The industry was becoming more sophisticated and calculated for capital spending and maintenance. However, a new $30,000 miniature golf course designed by Fairways Miniature Golds of Atlantic City was added in 1960 on the bluff overlooking the park. Events such as Pepsi Cola Day attracted crowds in May of each year, helping the park maintain its appeal and popularity. While the park remained mostly the same from year to year, new Skee-Ball alleys and food stands were added in 1967. To meet growing demand from the younger generation, WIXY hosted musician Neil Diamond at the park in August.

While the weather was not cooperative, thousands of guests stood in the rain to catch a glimpse of the singer. In addition to Neil Diamond, other headlining acts included Sonny and Cher and Paul Revere and the Raiders. The park's successful free concerts on weekend evenings were popular, but relied on guests paying to ride attractions for revenue. As the industry at large began to explore the idea of pay-one-price for all park attractions, Geauga Lake Park remained a pay as you go facility for participating in attractions. As Coney Island and Cedar Point reinvented themselves, it was decided that Geauga Lake was not going to be a gated and pay-one price-park.

Creating Funtime

The amusement park industry was growing from the inside and developing the next generation of leaders. One of those future leaders was Dale Van Voorhis, an auditor for Pricewaterhouse in Ohio. While at the Wharton School of Business completing his master's degree, Van Voorhis wrote a thesis on "The Internal Controls of Cash in an Amusement Park." In 1963, he was a featured speaker at the annual amusement industry convention in Chicago. Van Voorhis was intrigued by the industry, as his first job was selling cotton candy at Lake O'Springs Park when he was 14 years old. After that first summer, he moved over to Meyers

Lake Amusement Park working on the ground maintenance crew before working in games and later, the cash office. It was his time working in the cash office at Meyers Lake when he learned the ins and outs of basic accounting practices and running a financially sound business.

During his time at Pricewaterhouse, Gary Huffman, the treasurer of Pricewaterhouse, left for the same position at Cedar Point, leaving Van Voorhis shocked. The two talked frequently about the amusement industry and after Huffman started at Cedar Point, Van Voorhis received a call from Emil Legros who invited him to Cedar Point to join the accounting team. In the late 1960s, during a conversation with coworker Earl Gascoigne, Van Voorhis learned that coworkers Gascoigne, Gasper Lococo, and Milferd Jacobson attempted to purchase Geauga Lake Park but turned up unsuccessful. This time around, the newly assembled group was determined to find success of their own as amusement park owners.

All four individuals comprised quite the resume within the amusement park industry. Gascoigne, a former World War II Navy veteran, once taught business classes at Mount Union College before accepting a summer job at Cedar Point. He was a graduate of both Ohio's Miami and Kent University. After taking a liking to his seasonal position at Cedar Point and seeing great opportunity, he joined the Cedar Point management team full-time in 1963 as manager of Hotel Breakers. Two years later, he was promoted to marketing director where he oversaw all group sales, promotional activities, advertising, and public relations. At the time of Gascoigne's promotion to marketing director, Milford Jacobson was also appointed rides and amusement division manager and Gasper Lococo was overseeing the Cedar Point food-and-beverage division. Jacobson had been with Cedar Point for four years and previously worked in the operations department at both Disneyland in California and Freedomland in New York.

Dale Van Voorhis was the last of the group to join the team at Cedar Point. While working at Pricewaterhouse, Van Voorhis's former boss told him he knew the Schryer Family well and anytime he wished to meet them, to let him know. The group of Cedar Point executives now with Van Voorhis, re-approached the Schryer Family about purchasing Geauga Lake. Negotiations for purchasing the park began in October 1967 and continued through 1968 with an agreement being signed one year after negotiations began. As purchase negotiations continued for Geauga Lake Park, one of the biggest days in the park's history through the 1960s occurred on August 1, 1968, for WIXY Appreciation Day. Charles Schryer explained to the newspapers that 100,000 people were on hand for the event and the parking lot was packed. A teenager show featuring Gene Pitney, The Amboy Dukes, Peppermint Troller Company and Jay & the Techniques brought in 83 buses from Cleveland.

The new ownership group purchased the park, the 55-acre lake, and over 300 acres of property for $1.5 million. The group of former Cedar Point executives worked with the Ohio Company from Columbus, Ohio, to raise the necessary funds. The Ohio Company, owned by the Wolfe Family, also helped establish Riverside Park, later renamed Columbus Zoo. The agreement saw the Schryer's receive half the money up front for the park and the rest of the money over the next seven years. After the sales agreement was signed, the Schryer brothers met with the new owners and introduced them to the existing team and to tour the facility. When the park was sold, Ann Schryer agreed to stay involved at the park to help with the transition of ownership. When she and the rest of her family retired from the amusement industry, the new ownership group awarded each previous owner with their own lifetime pass. The 1968 season was on par with past years, but moving forward, Geauga Lake Park would undergo significant upgrades and general improvements not seen before. A new era of fun was about to be introduced at Geauga Lake Park.

Funtime Partners L-R:
Dale Van Voorhis,
Milferd Jacobson,
Gasper Lococo,
Earl Gascoigne

The photo at the top of the page is the first in a series of photographs that were taken for park management in 1925. This is indicated by the number shown at the bottom right corner.

The photo at the bottom of the page shows the refreshment stand located inside the parks original arcade.

Geauga Lake

Baseball fields and athletic fields were once major attractions at amusement parks. These fields offered space to host a variety of activities including games for children and adults; many of which were free of charge. The presence of athletic fields fostered social interaction and enhanced the overall appeal of the park beyond the amusement rides.

Row boats remained a popular attraction on the lake

The Circle Swing, quickly became a popular attraction upon its debut in 1925. The photo to the left shows the ride with its original ride vehicles. When new stainless-steel rocket ride vehicles were added to the ride in the 1930s from the R.E. Chambers Company, the ride was renamed the Rockets Ships.

This photo captures what was then the end of the parks midway.
To the left is the Whip

The Cuddle Up was a popular ride at the park until its final season in 1983.

A bird's-eye view of the midway from the Sky Rocket, showing the same section of the midway as seen in the photo above.

The Tumble Bug, later renamed The Bug was manufactured by Traver Engineering Company. Five ride vehicles traveled over the circular track featuring two hills. During the first eight years of ownership under the Schryer Family, $500,000 was invested into the park with new attractions and facades such as the one shown in the top photo.

When Sky Rocket was renamed the Clipper, the park also introduced new closed front trains. At one point in time, the rides second hill superstructure facing the parking lot featured large letters reading 'Geauga Lake Park.'

The Tumble Bug, later renamed The Bug was manufactured by Traver Engineering Company. Five ride vehicles traveled over the circular track featuring two hills. During the first eight years of ownership under the Schryer Family, $500,000 was invested into the park with new attractions and facades such as the one shown in the top photo.

When Sky Rocket was renamed the Clipper, the park also introduced new closed front trains. At one point in time, the rides second hill superstructure facing the parking lot featured large letters reading 'Geauga Lake Park.'

The park featured various food and games stands. While the park owned and operated all of the rides and food stands, a number of concessionaires continued to operate the games and other amusements. To meet the demand for games of chance, game concessionaires purchased $100,000 worth of prizes each season.

The park featured a number of junior or kiddie sized rides for children. Many of these sized down rides remained in operation for decades and later called Rainbow Island home.

Mike Funyak

Geauga Lake

The Whip remained in operation until the 1970s when it was removed for newer attractions. Notice the power lines and transformers by and over the ride. By today's standards, amusement rides are not permitted to operate under or within 15 feet of power lines.

A long line of guests await their turn to board the Tilt-a-Whirl on a summer day. The Fun House is the building located next to the Tilt-a-Whirl. The taller part of the building's roof is to accommodate the slide inside the Fun House.

The Roll-O-Plane, manufacturing by the Eyerly Aircraft Company, operated at the park for a brief period compared to its counterparts that the park purchased from the company.

Various midway games such as the Fish Pond could be found in the Arcade.

Surprise in the Dark as seen in the 1950s was a dark ride manufactured by the Pretzel Amusement Company.

Midway crowd around the Loop-O-Plane

The Olympic-sized Swimming Pool was the site where Johnny Weissmuller broke the world record in the 220-yard freestyle.

Little Dipper was located in the area that eventually anchored a new Kiddieland and later Turtle Beach, both developed by Funtime ownership and management.

This artwork appeared on the park's letterhead during the 1940s

CHAPTER 3

The Funtime Era
1969-1980

The new owners of Geauga Lake Park called themselves Funtime Incorporated. Earl Gascoigne was named president, Gasper Lococo and Milford Jacobson were named vice presidents, and Dale Van Voorhis named secretary-treasurer. As the new company prepared for the 1969 season, Earl Gascoigne discussed with George Milay about an opportunity to build an animal marine park on the opposite side of the lake from Geauga Lake Park. Milay previously considered building a second marine park west of Sandusky, near Port Clinton. What Milay didn't know originally was the land being proposed for his new animal marine park was owned by Cedar Point. Gascoigne, who took a liking to the San Diego Sea World park, suggested the idea to Milay in 1966, but the marine park in Sandusky never materialized. Gascoigne convinced Milay to build his park next to Geauga Lake because of the proximity to the turnpike and population of the area. The 50-acre property that became Sea World of Ohio was sold to George Milay for the same price per acre that Funtime paid. The marketing potential for both parks was endless, and Gascoigne knew the idea would help both facilities become popular with families. Construction for Sea World began in the spring of 1969. In a November 21, 1968, *Cleveland Plain Dealer* article, Milay explained:

> *"The new park will feature some of the most popular and successful shows and exhibits which we now have at Sea World in San Diego. We plan to construct a stadium for a combination killer whale and dolphin show, a stadium for a penguin and sea lion show and several smaller static exhibits such as freshwater dolphins and seals."*

In 1968, Geauga Lake Park broke even, and in the first year of the Funtime ownership, the park made a profit. This was in large part due to the almost $1 million improvements invested into the park in 1969. The most noticeable addition was the monorail, one of six new rides added. Other new rides included a new Ferris Wheel and two children's attractions. New paint was added to buildings, and walkways saw the addition of new blacktop. The Clipper was also renamed Big Dipper. Unfortunately, the first day on which the park was to open, three inches of snow covered on the grounds, leading to park closure. The rest of the season however, was deemed successful. When asked about the operating season for a June 2, 1969 article in the *Cleveland Press*, Earl Gascoigne explained:

> *"Our master plan covers five years of concentrated effort. For the present, we're working hard to provide the best possible clean as a whistle family fun spot we can"*

The optimism of the 1969 summer season paved the way for a bright future at Geauga Lake. However, the same could not be said for Euclid Beach Park in Cleveland, as 1969 marked its final season. The expected closing of the 75-acre Euclid Beach Park was a major turning point for the local market in and around Cleveland. Rumors of the park closing echoed through the community and amusement industry for a few years. The Humphrey Family operated their amusement park based on heritage from the early days and struggled to evolve with the times. Prior to 1969, Euclid Beach had encountered multiple difficulties such as removing structures and selling rides. One ride in particular, the American Racing Derby, was sold in 1967 to Cedar Point.

Unfortunately, the Humphrey Family chose not to evolve with the ever-changing times. The idea of gating Euclid Beach Park — or as guests referred to it, "The Beach" — and charging admission was not even a possibility by Dudley Humphrey III or his family as they were against an admission fee to enter the park. One of the most popular and visited parks within the industry had said goodbye. It was a grim reminder that even successful enterprises could close, even after years of success. The park's departure occurred only two years after the closing of another popular and successful amusement park, Riverview Park located outside Chicago, Illinois. Time changes, people change, and markets shift and gravitate to new tastes and expectations, but guest loyalty is equally important. When Euclid Beach Park closed, guests who previously patronized Euclid Beach had two decisions: they chose either to visit either Cedar Point or Geauga Lake. For many area residents, Geauga Lake became the preferred choice. After the closing of Euclid Beach Park, the Humphrey Family was determined to pack up as many park rides and equipment as possible to refocus their efforts and open a new amusement park elsewhere. In June 1969, the Humphrey Family purchased 64 acres in Portage County near Streetsboro to construct a new amusement park called Shady Lake Park. Construction on the new park even started prior to the final operating day of Euclid Beach Park, but the project was delayed for a number of years.

The Geauga Lake Adventure

When Sea World of Ohio opened in 1970, the new marine park attracted 5,500 visitors on opening day and 1.1 million visitors during its first operating season. Eventually Sea World purchased additional property from Funtime Incorporated and grew the park to 232 acres in size. An agreement between Funtime Inc and Milay was drafted that Geauga Lake would not have any entertainment shows and Sea World would not add amusement rides. Two years after the agreement was signed, Milay sued Funtime to break the agreement. After settling the disagreement, the two parks worked hand in hand to market their respective parks.

Between Sea World and Geauga Lake, the two parks combined to hire up to 4,000 and 5,000 individuals each summer. The Funtime five-year business plan for Geauga Lake was simple; invest at least $1 million into the park each season. With the help of the Ohio Company, Funtime was able to produce the necessary funding needed to guarantee the business plan became reality. Five attractions were added to the park's lineup for 1970: Himalaya, Tilt-a-Whirl, Flying Scooter, Spider, and Trabant. Additionally, the park purchased ride vehicles from Euclid Beach Park's Bug to help with ongoing maintenance.

The 1970s were growing years for Geauga Lake, as the park was quite small and retained its small traditional park charm. The new Funtime ownership group committed to retain the traditions, appeal, and charm of the park yet added rides, games, and amusements that appealed to multiple generations of visitors. Murray Goldberg, owner of Progressive Amusements, a games concession company since the 1930s, was contracted under a 10-year lease to own and operate games around the Big Dipper beginning in 1969. Goldberg was a true showman and developed scales for the Guess Your Weight game for the Century of Progress exhibition in Chicago in 1933-1934. He also operated games at the Great Lakes Exposition in 1936-1937, and at the New York World's Fair in 1939-1940. Goldberg established Geauga Lake as a games park, in that the park featured games set up in true showmen or boardwalk style. This referred to the game operators calling in participants and encouraging park goers to step up and play games in order to win a prize. A strong and charismatic game operator could make a lot of money during any given operating day, especially since game operators were paid on commission.

As the park moved into the 1970s, new attractions such as the Sky Glide, Paratrooper, and Round Up opened, as did the Wharf Restaurant, where fish and chicken were served to popular fanfare. With the addition of new rides, older rides were evaluated yearly, and it was determined the Wild Mouse would be removed. The ride's final year came in 1971 and was later sold to nearby Chippewa Lake Park. Another ride that disappeared in the early 1970s was the park's dark ride known at the time as Surprise in the Dark which gave way for additional arcade games. While the park continued to modernize, ownership continued to retain many of the park's older rides. Annual park enhancements also included new

revenue generating opportunities, such as unveiling art opportunities for guests. Tricia Kaman opened her first Pastel Portrait stand at Geauga Lake in 1971 and later expanded her operation to include a Fun Photo spot at the park starting in 1976 followed by Antique Photos. The partnership between Kaman and Geauga Lake management added further value to the overall guest and family experience at the park.

At the same time, a new logo that became synonymous with the Funtime era of Geauga Lake debuted. 1972 saw the beginning of a newly redesigned main entrance gate and the opening of the $180,000 Merry Old-Mobiles antique car ride from Arrow Development, along with the $500,000 Gold Rush log flume and its 40-foot splashdown. The Gold Rush log flume was manufactured by Japanese company, Sansei. Interestingly enough, the blueprints for this ride were printed backwards in Japanese. Although leading to a challenge for the maintenance team, the two new rides proved to be quite popular with families. The opening of these rides expanded the park's footprint and created what eventually became known as Western Village. The new 40-acre section of the park was styled in the architecture of the Western Reserve that predominated in Northeastern Ohio in the late 1800s. The new rides were designed to preserve and enhance the natural wooded look of the property. Families were also encouraged to try their luck at

The park not only unveiled a new main entrance in 1972 but two attractions popular with families: the Merry Oldies antique cars and Gold Rush log flume.

the Bonanza electronic shooting gallery, where-in once targets were hit, things really happened. Additionally for the youngest guests, Forest Funland petting farm was unveiled as a new location for children and families to visit barnyard animals. Other additions included a new gift shop, food stand and restroom facility. Encouraged by growth in popularity and patronage, the park extended its operating hours both during the week and on weekends.

By 1973, park revenue jumped to $4.1 million with overall profits growing to $414,000. This was the season in which the park moved from a ride ticket system to strictly a pay-one-price plan. The two-year project for completing the new main entrance was also unveiled on opening day 1973. Built to accommodate growing attendance, the newly opened main entrance's location helped bridge the gap between the older park and expanded western area of the park. By the end of the operating season, management determined that 1974 capital expenditures would be financed out of cash flow instead of borrowing. Plans for 1974 saw the popular Spaghetti House restaurant double in size, three food stands added, and two additional picnic shelters were built. The park continued to cater to families by adding the Big Ditch boat adventure, where riders were taken into a trough cut through Geauga Lake passing themed displays. And the Skyline of the park changed forever with the addition of the 15-story Skyscraper observation tower in 1974. Guests now had the opportunity to see the amusement park from 200 feet in the sky, but also the incredible view it offered of the lake and surrounding area.

Along with the Big Dipper, the Skyscraper became one of the most noticeable park icons for travelers. One of the park's other noteworthy attractions, the Carousel, received a major refurbishment and looked better than ever when it reopened in 1974 with new paint and 500 lights. Additionally, the Big Dipper received a major refurbishment project. One night park management heard loud unusual screams coming from the ride. Upon arriving at the ride, it was discovered a piece of track broke causing the roller coaster train to come to a screeching halt. Fortunately, no one was injured, but the incident initiated a multiple-year project for the ride. By 1976, the Big Dipper was entirely rebuilt with new wood and painted white.

Admission to Geauga Lake was priced 2/3 or 60% of the price of Cedar Point. The main driver for the Funtime ownership group was to provide a low-cost alternative for families and attract group business. Every park looked at industry trends and the industry at large to see what worked and did not work. For Geauga Lake, the park was in a prime position to compete for a large market in Northeastern Ohio. The competition was not just Cedar Point, but other nearby amusement parks such as Meyer's Lake Amusement Park in Canton and even Idora Park in Youngstown, Ohio. Waldameer Park, Conneaut Lake Park, and even Kennywood near Pittsburgh, Pennsylvania, were also deemed competition, mainly due to the turnpike. And while Geauga Lake continued to invest heavily in new rides, food and game operations, the park always made every effort to attract families with their marketing efforts. In wanting to help promote the family atmosphere of the park and meet growing demand, a group of costumed characters called The Fun Bunch were introduced in 1975. Geauga Dog, introduced three years prior, led this group of fun ambassadors. The Fun Bunch were eagerly embraced by park visitors, especially popular with children. The other Fun Bunch characters included Dandy Lion, Penny Panda, and Gunky Monkey.

By the mid-1970s, roller coasters had re-entered the picture as being major attractions for amusement parks. The park already featured a popular wooden roller coaster, but steel roller coasters were becoming the talk of the amusement industry. Efforts led by the engineering team at Arrow Development proved steel roller coasters could not only be popular with families, but take riders upside down. Following an invitation from Arrow Development to see their latest roller coaster design called the Corkscrew, Dale Van Voorhis, Jim Meikle, and Elmer Tucek traveled to the company's headquarters to review plans and ride

The Fun Bunch: Gunky Monkey, Dandy Lion, Penny Panda, and Geauga Dog

the prototype attraction. Meikle, another former Cedar Point employee, began his career in the amusement industry at the age of 14. He eventually rose to the position of president of operations before joining the team at Geauga Lake in a similar role in 1971. Tucek was the park's maintenance director, who for almost 45 years at that point had worked at Geauga Lake repairing rides.

Deciding the hefty price tag of $700,000 was too steep for a prototype attraction, park officials elected to not make the purchase. Instead, Knott's Berry Farm in California made the purchase, unveiling the first Corkscrew roller coaster of its kind to the general public. Instead of that costlier roller coaster, the Geauga Lake team added the Zyclone roller coaster, replacing the Little Dipper in 1976. Designed by Italian ride manufacturer, Pinfari, the new Zyclone stood 40 feet tall and featured 1,400 feet of track.

The amusement industry by this time embraced the European amusement ride market, and like other parks, Geauga Lake slowly began adding these types of rides. In comparison to the American amusement ride market, the European rides featured exciting flash that drew attention unlike the American built rides. While many of these European rides were simply enhanced versions of U.S. counterparts, they created a new dynamic to the overall amusement park experience. These rides also enabled the park to take a chance on installing portable or moveable rides to see if they were popular with guests. If deemed necessary, the flexibility of moving the ride elsewhere and even removing the ride altogether proved to be a popular decision among many parks. At this point in time, the park featured 33 major rides and 17 kiddie rides and looked ahead to adding other major attractions. Between 1975 and 1976, Geauga Lake spent $3 million on adding European rides such as the Calypso, Music Express, Super Cat, and Matterhorn.

New European attractions were not the only area in which the park spent over $1 million. By 1976, general liability specialty insurance for amusement parks continued to rise, hurting the industry at large, causing some park owners to cease operations. At one point, management struggled finding an insurer because the park had to have $1 million of coverage. When negotiations broke down, Geauga Lake management asked Harry Henninger Jr., general manager of Kennywood, to help with securing a policy. Henninger was able to help with sourcing and contacting companies who were able to provide Geauga Lake with an insurance provider, allowing them to operate for the season.

All For Fun

With the success of the Corkscrew, Arrow Development introduced what they promoted as the double looping coaster in 1976. Driven by its uniqueness, the Geauga Lake team decided to purchase a roller coaster featuring two consecutive loops. When the Double Loop debuted in 1977, it was an immediate success; it was the first double-looping coaster in the world. Domestic and international guests from miles away visited the park and were impressed with the new roller coaster. The ride reached heights of 90 feet and sent riders through two vertical loops of 65 and 55 feet. The introduction of the Double Loop expanded this new area of the park and replaced the Forest Funland. It was at this time the area became known as Western Village. The previously unused and undeveloped area of

the park had now transformed the park into a modern-day amusement park with themed elements. It would not be long until additional rides moved into this area of the park, such as the Scrambler and Fly-O-Plane. It also left the possibility for the addition of even larger attractions in the future. Western Village was greatly enhanced by the addition of the Double Loop and other new amusements, such as Earl's Arcade, named for Park President Earl Gascoigne with 28 Skee-Ball machines added, as were additional midway games. A new snack stand, candy story, gift shop, pottery shop, and sketch artist stand also opened. Previously, the park added the Gold Rush Theatre for live entertainment from the Fun Bunch and other stage shows.

Elsewhere in the park, the former Fun House was converted into the Palace Theater. The $125,000 renovation project transformed the building into an 800-seat, air-conditioned theater with wall-to-wall carpeting. The new Palace Theater featured shows with a three-piece band performing 28 songs. Other entertainment in the park consisted of a new seven-minute puppet show with recorded calliope music on the midway. Each day at 5:00 p.m., a parade featured the park's Fun Bunch. As became customary for Geauga Lake, park beautification was not limited, even with the addition of the $1.3 million Double Loop roller coaster. Deemed vital to the park's reputation, brick planters, blacktopping, fencing, guard rails, and trashcans were added throughout the park. One of the primary areas of focus during the Funtime era was the overall perception and image of the park. While the park was never rundown or unsafe, the company hoped to attract individuals who may not have visited for several years or attract new families in the hope of repeat business. The idea was simple, to impress guests upon entering the park, with not only the park attractions, but the overall presentation of the park and its courteous employees.

Attendance grew slowly in the 1970s and rightfully so. The popular pay-one-price option — commonly referred to as P.O.P. — helped increase revenue and plan for future investments. In 1975, attendance sat at 739,000, increased to 760,000 in 1976 and then grew by 14% to 870,000 in 1977. The annual increase in attendance forced the park to increase the number of parking spaces to accommodate up to 5,000 vehicles. During the mid-to-late 1970s, 42% of the park's attendance stemmed from school and group business. This guaranteed money helped with the park's annual improvement projects plus provided a kick-back to employees with end-of-the-year bonuses. The park began offering employees a 15 cents per hour bonus for every hour worked toward the end of the operating season. By 1977, the park had 37 full-time employees; at summer's peak there were 455 including all seasonal positions.

Pay-one-price tickets cost $5.95 for adults and children 4 and older. This option gave guests unlimited access to rides and entertainment. Schools, youth groups, and senior citizens were offered generous discounts and children under 4 were admitted free. A similar admission system was offered across the lake at Sea World, where it cost $5.95 for adults, $4.25 for children ages 4 to 12 and children under 4 were free. Combined, Geauga Lake and Sea World offered great entertainment for everyone in the family. In 1977, it was estimated that 30% of the more than 1 million visitors for the combined parks came from the Greater Pittsburgh area across the state line in Pennsylvania. Motel and hotel accommodations were also reasonable for families, leading many to stay multiple days to enjoy both parks. Gascoigne's vision of a thriving entertainment resort at Geauga Lake was now reality.

Growing Attendance

Encouraged by the success of the Double Loop, management approached Arrow Development about purchasing a Corkscrew for the following season. Taking a portion of the park's parking lot for buses and campers, the Corkscrew was unveiled in the summer of 1978. The best of the old and new were evident as travelers approached the park with the Corkscrew located next to the Big Dipper roller coaster. $1.9 million was spent improving the park, which included modifications to the parking lot, new and enhanced food operation facilities, a new water tower, new ticket booths, facility painting, and widening of the park midways. As the park had done in previous years, the addition of newer attractions gave way to the removal of older attractions. Guests noticed that the Bug, which had been a park staple for 50 years, was removed. In its place was the Trabant. The park also relocated the Spider to the west side of the Corkscrew. Additionally, the price of admission increased to $6.50. Geauga Lake could now market itself as the first park in Ohio to have two looping roller coasters, a feat Cedar Point could not promote.

The promotion of roller coasters at parks began to ramp up at parks all over the United States. Kings Island emerged as a major player in the Ohio amusement park market and invested heavily in new attractions. While other amusement

parks in Ohio could not invest in the likes of Geauga Lake, Kings Island, or Cedar Point, it was only a matter of time before they could no longer attract crowds. Meyers Lake Amusement Park in Canton, Ohio, ceased operations in 1974, while other parks like LeSourdsville Lake and Idora Park in Youngstown remained in operation. Cincinnati's Coney Island ownership group, which had been a major player in the industry, had sold to Taft Broadcasting in the late 1960s, operating Coney Island through 1971 until Kings Island opened. The new park led by Coney's former owners reinvented the amusement park industry and created the modern-day theme park in the region, which took the industry by storm. As this was occurring, Cedar Point in Sandusky, Ohio, was slowly growing and preparing itself for a new chapter in its history.

Additionally, after years of delays, the Humphrey Family opened their new amusement park, Shady Lake Park in nearby Streetsboro, Ohio. Only a mere nine miles from Geauga Lake and not even a 30-minute commute by car, the new amusement park proved no real competition for Geauga Lake. While the Humphrey Family originally planned to rebuild the Thriller from Euclid Beach, Shady Lake had no direct impact on the future development of Geauga Lake. Although Shady Lake Park was a successful venture, a family dispute led to its closure at the end of the 1982 summer season.

In the mid-1970s, the thought of an amusement owner and operator owning multiple parks was making a comeback in the industry. In the years to come, this would have a direct impact on not just the industry, but Geauga Lake as well. Funtime Inc. reached an agreement to expand its amusement park operation by acquiring Familyland Amusement Center in Lake Delton, Wisconsin. The deal eventually fell through as Funtime took an option on a 185-acre site just south of Ann Arbor, Michigan, as a possible location for a new amusement park. At the same time, Cedar Point Inc, the owners of Cedar Point, attempted to acquire land 50 miles west of Detroit, Michigan, for a possible new amusement park. The project later moved to sites in the Battle Creek, Kalamazoo area but similar to Funtime, no amusement park was ever built. Then in 1978, Cedar Point purchased Valley Fair, an amusement park located in Shakopee, Minnesota. This was the beginning of a major development for not just Cedar Point and its parent company's operation, but the industry at large.

Similar to Coney Island, Chippewa Lake Park was purchased by a publicly owned company in 1969. Continental Business Enterprises developed plans to transform Chippewa Lake Park into more of a summer resort. Public interest in the project did not gather much excitement. Being that Chippewa Lake Park was now owned by a public company, annual reports for the company's shareholders were distributed annually, and on the back of the Continental Business Enterprises annual report was the list of the groups that visited Chippewa Lake Park. Other parks such as Geauga Lake eventually attracted those groups. Without the steady income generated from those industrial and large groups, Chippewa Lake Park closed forever following the 1978 season. The Chippewa Lake Park property was abandoned, leaving an eyesore for the community of Medina, Ohio. As the Geauga Lake ownership team at the time believed, Chippewa was owned and operated by people who didn't know what they were doing, and had no business being in the amusement park industry. But while Chippewa Lake Park was owned by a publicly traded company, so was Geauga Lake. Funtime Inc. had quietly become a publicly owned company in the early 1970s by listing itself on the NASDAQ stock exchange. While other nearby amusement parks struggled to survive, attendance figures at Geauga Lake continued to rise. In 1978, attendance was up over 20% from the 870,000 guests who visited the park in 1977. Spending on food increased dramatically and in a September 16, 1978 Amusement Business article on the park, Gascoigne shared:

> "It seems no matter how many food stands we open, they all do well without affecting existing stands. There will definitely be continued expansion of the food operation."

During the latter part of the decade, the park expanded its marketing campaign to reach Detroit, Columbus, and western Pennsylvania. Gascoigne, whose background was in marketing, strategized a plan with Vice President of Sales Ron Adams to wait to draw people from a distance until Geauga Lake had a strong product. The idea was that those first-time guests would be impressed and return. Gascogine experimented with a free ticket giveaway late in the 1978 season. Inserts were placed in a test market newspaper containing four free admission passes through August 21 and Labor Day. In return for the admission tickets, the newspaper gave the park a full-page ad for free. Even prior to this creative promotion, the park saw record crowds when 24,104 guests entered the park on August 13, surpassing the previous record of 22,000 from 1975. While the park administration liked what they saw on paper with record attendance days, an influx of visitors at one time was taxing on the staff and the facility. The park also operated the ballroom year-round for private parties along with the Our Famous Recipe chicken restaurant located adjacent to the park. Elsewhere, the Meyers Lake Park Ballroom was destroyed by a fire, which became a common theme for abandoned structures at amusement parks. The fire at Meyers Lake reminded locals of the importance the park had on the community. And like Chippewa Lake, both parks' popular roller coasters stood abandoned as a reminder of many happy summer memories. With the ongoing success of Geauga Lake, the people of Aurora and Bainbridge Township could never imagine anything similar happening to Geauga Lake or Sea World.

The gasoline shortage of the late 1970s did not help businesses, especially destination locations or mini-vacation spots that Geauga Lake and Sea World were considered. While the park did add a new ride, the Enterprise to the Western Village, other improvements to the park were kept to a minimum. A new Dodgem bumper car 4,000-square-foot building opened next to the Enterprise that same season. In addition, a new $20,000 pumping system to provide water to the Western Village area fire hydrants and for hosing of the midways was needed. While the gasoline shortage provided setbacks, inclement weather during the summer

of 1979 impacted business even more. Cooler temperatures and rain cut attendance at not just Geauga Lake but other parks throughout northeastern Ohio and western Pennsylvania. The park had an obligation to make payments owed on the Corkscrew and Double Loop.

Ultimately wanting to introduce a new attraction, it was decided to purchase a non-amusement ride, the Cinema 180, featuring a wraparound screen under a domed structure. Also, there was a focus on rebuilding and preserving one of the park's most beloved attractions, the Big Dipper. The ride was rebuilt with pressure treated wood and was not repainted but stained after a few seasons. At a cost of $800,000, the entire structure after the first hill was dismantled to the ground and rebuilt. One major and noticeable modification during the rebuilding of the ride was the removal of the double dip.

The 1980 season was relatively quiet, but did see the introduction of the end-of-season Oktoberfest event. A trip by Dale Van Voorhis with his wife Bonnie, to Germany's Oktoberfest fueled the idea to have a similar event at Geauga Lake. The event was originally not successful for Geauga Lake and did not gross a profit for the event's first three years. Eventually Oktoberfest became extremely successful and popular with management. The new event helped attract guests to the latter half of the park's operating season and provided guests with another reason to visit for a second time.

Weather was much better in 1980 versus 1979 and the park saw record attendance once again. Following the end of the season, the park removed the Zyclone, Geauga Queen miniature train, Giant Slide, Paratrooper, Bayern Kurve, and Round Up. The removal of rides and attractions is never a good sign, but with the economic downturn in guest spending and traveling, the removal of attractions was a necessary one for future development, especially if the park was to attract guests from outside Bainbridge Township and Aurora, Ohio.

> "Where do you go when you're looking for fun, for the kids, for you, for everyone, Geauga Lake's the place. The Double Loop, for Corkscrew too, for ride and thrills just made for you, Geauga Lake's the place. Want a hundred rides and things to do in Aurora, Ohio, there's a place for you. Geauga Lake's the place. Make no mistake Geauga Lake is as much fun as you can take, Geauga Lake's the place."
>
> —*1979 TV Commercial Jingle*

During the Funtime era, Geauga Lake billboards became a common scene along major highways advertising the park as a great place for family fun.

Mike Funyak

New attractions such the Big Ditch and Sky Glide proved to be popular attractions. Opening in 1973, Big Ditch was a Disney-like attraction that featured props and western themed scenes. The last scene of the ride featured a boat torn open with a man hanging from a chandelier. The Big Ditch closed after the 1985 season and the Sky Glide in 1993.

Geauga Lake

Mike Funyak

John Miller who designed the Fun House, worked closely with Aurel Vaszin of Dayton Fun House and Riding Device Manufacturing to supply the attractions machinery including the Barrel of Fun.

Geauga Lake

The Zyclone (top) and Super Cat (bottom)

Mike Funyak

Geauga Lake

Mike Funyak

Geauga Lake

Mike Funyak

Before gaining a greater presence in the amusement industry, Tricia Kaman opened her first pastel portrait stand at Geauga Lake in 1971. The success at Geauga Lake, helped Kaman open similar art stands at Idlewild Park in Ligonier, Pennsylvania in 1975, and later Kennywood Park in West Mifflin, Pennsylvania in 1979. During the 1970s, Kaman also introduced Fun Photo and Antique Photo stands at Geauga Lake.

As Geauga Lake developed and grew in popularity, so did Sea World on the opposite side of the lake.

Kiddieland

Western Village Midway

CHAPTER 4

Marketing Genius
1981-1994

In August of 1980, an inspection of the structural integrity of the Carousel building was completed, and it was discovered the structure was in far worse condition than originally believed. At the conclusion of the season, the attraction was quickly dismantled, and the building was razed. Plans for a new location and ride pavilion were quickly put into motion. The original Carousel building, which dated back to 1925, was a classic structure that took advantage of the shoreline and offered a food stand on the lower level of the building. A new pavilion was built and added to the park in Western Village to house the refurbished Carousel for the following season. While reviewing other attractions from the 1920s, it was decided to renovate the park's arcade. The lone attraction that remained now from the 1925 season along the shoreline was the Rocket Ships. To help fill the void of the removed attractions alongside the lake, the park added two from Chance Rides: a Rotor and Yo-Yo.

On December 23, 1981, Funtime Inc. agreed to purchase 50% of the business that owned and operated Darien Lake in Buffalo, New York. The owner of Darien Lake at the time, Paul Synder, sought out Funtime as an equal partner because of the success of Geauga Lake. The opportunity to expand operations by owning and operating two separate amusement parks put Funtime Incorporated in the same conversation as the newly formed Cedar Fair, which owned and operated Cedar Point and Valleyfair. Darien Lake offered different opportunities unseen at Geauga Lake. Darien Lake held not only an amusement park, but also a waterpark and campground located on 1,250 acres. While Darien Lake began as a campground in 1964, amusement rides arrived in 1980 as Snyder used his facility to showcase attractions manufactured by the now named Arrow-Huss. This was the successor company of Arrow Development, which designed the Geauga Lake Double Loop and Corkscrew. Darien Lake featured 30 rides, including a new looping roller coaster, and a massive 2,000-site camping facility. One of the first changes implemented by Funtime at Darien Lake was the introduction of games and retail operations. Eventually, improvements and additions were made to the water attractions that started to become popular within the industry. At the same time, Gasper Lococo was named president and chief operating officer for Darien Lake in the new partnership.

For Geauga Lake, 1982 was a quiet season with no new additions or rides. Plans for a new amphitheater were abandoned due to opposition from local residents. And by the end of the summer season, attendance dropped 14% below the record number set in 1980. Parks began turning toward new avenues to spark interest in visitation, and that included means outside of adding new amusement attractions. At the beginning of the new decade, the amusement park and waterpark industry had integrated into one business. George Milay, who created the marine park concept with Sea World, innovated and opened Florida's Wet 'n Wild in 1977. Many individuals credit Milay with opening and creating the modern-day waterpark with the opening of Wet 'n Wild. Geauga Lake saw this as an opportunity to do something innovative, but first it took someone with a vision.

Drench Dried Fun

In August 1982, Dale Van Voorhis was elected president and CEO of Funtime Inc. Past President Earl Gascoigne left his position but remained active in the amusement industry. In the years to come, Gascoigne found himself operating arcade games at Old Indiana Amusement Park and later as elected president of the International Association of Amusement Parks and Attractions (IAAPA) in 1985. In a company letter dated December 21, 1982, Van Voorhis announced:

> *"We will have an important announcement to make regarding the installation of a major new attraction at the park which will add a wonderful new dimension to the Geauga Lake entertainment center."*

The announcement called for the $1.5 million addition of a full-scale waterpark dubbed Boardwalk Shores. Never before did an amusement park commit to having both amusement rides and waterpark attractions for the same price. When Boardwalk Shores opened, attendance jumped back up 14%, rising significantly to 915,000 visitors in 1983. The park's creative marketing approach in 1983 was designed to attract families in the way of offering a quality mini-vacation at a great value for the price of $9.95 a person.

To accommodate space for the new Boardwalk Shores, the Flying Scooters and Rocket Ships were relocated next to the Corkscrew. Neptune Falls and the Undertow slide complex was an immediate success and featured four twisting,

interlocking body water slides, each 400 feet in length, 46 feet high with 360 degree turns and 45-degree drops. Each slide emptied into a 22-foot by 52-foot splash pool. A 20-foot kiddie slide with nine slides emptying into the lake was also added, as were four kiddie pools. To make the sandy beach suitable for swimming, the park had to dredge 16 to 18 feet of silt to reach the lake bottom, and underwater pilings were required to be installed to stabilize the hundreds of tons of sand being installed at the bottom of the beach. The new water attractions overlooked the shoreline of Geauga Lake. Found within the new Boardwalk Shores was a refurbished Wharf Restaurant and a portion of the park's former ballroom converted into a bathhouse. The opening of Boardwalk Shores also gave guests access to the beach for the first time in many years, and its location was ideal, given its proximity to the lake and Big Dipper.

The introduction of water slides at a traditional amusement park was unusual. When log flume attractions started to be installed at parks, some park owners had a negative perception on what it would mean for the industry at large. When Geauga Lake permitted swimsuits as acceptable park attire in that season, it was believed this might encourage bad behavior from park guests. Boardwalk Shores was only the beginning for the park's new venture into the waterpark business.

However, the opening of Boardwalk Shores was overshadowed by two unfortunate incidents. On July 20, 1983, an electrical worker with an outside contractor was electrocuted while performing work on the park's Parkview Express monorail attraction, and the following month, an incident occurred when a female rider was thrown 25 feet from the Fly-O-Plane. The guest suffered a broken collarbone and injuries to her back and right ankle. The ride was closed immediately and during the ensuing court case, it was argued that the ride operator failed to secure the ride vehicle door before starting the ride. When the ride vehicle or the plane turned, the door flew open, ejecting one rider and forcing the co-rider to hold on for their life. The park was found liable, and a settlement occurred with $150,000 in damages awarded to the injured rider and $15,500 to the other rider. After the incident, the ride was removed from the park and never operated again.

While the park encountered some unfortunate situations, Geauga Lake continued to enjoy success with its shoulder-season event, Oktoberfest. The event grew in size each year and featured popular entertainers such as "The Polka King" Frank Yankovic and over 200 nearby vendors. The event also attracted numerous sponsors. In 1983, Family Nights were introduced as part of Oktoberfest with a $10 carload special for guests. Prior to the 1983 season, park ownership recognized a need to increase marketing efforts to increase revenue. Marketing found inside the park was enhanced with the installation of 47 closed circuit televisions in specific locations. Commercials from paid advertisers were featured, as were advertisements on park activities, events, and previews for in-park entertainment and public service announcements. This investment was considered unique and proved to be another successful venture, allowing creativity to push the business forward.

It was determined the park needed to start the search for a marketing manager who could help unleash creativity and spark a decade of marketing genius for the park. Later that same year in October, one of Van Voorhis's first personnel decisions was to hire Gasper Lococo's nephew, Jeff Lococo, who was no stranger to the amusement industry. Previously, Jeff worked at Cedar Point in maintenance while in high school and from 1979 to 1982 as a sales manager at Marriott's Great America near Chicago, Illinois. With Jeff onboard, Geauga Lake entered a decade in which most people recall as the most original and innovative. Jeff made an instant impact on the marketing campaign for Geauga Lake and was promoted to marketing director one year after joining the Geauga Lake team. The park's television commercials, newspaper advertisements, and group sales materials were wildly popular, memorable, and continued for the next decade.

In 1984, Geauga Lake unveiled The Wave. The Wave, the only authentic tsunami wave pool in the Midwest, was the second-largest wave pool in the United States and first of its kind to create a four-six-foot, ocean-like surf wave, roughly every five minutes. The Wave occupied one and three-quarters acres and used 1,780,000 gallons of water and cost $2 million to construct. Jeff Lococo and a small team discovered a tsunami wave pool in Tempe, Arizona, and believed a wave pool of its kind would be the perfect fit for the newly added Boardwalk Shores section of Geauga Lake. The Wave was designed and manufactured by WaveTek of Mansfield, Ohio. Originally supposed to feature a pneumatic system, the operating system was actually a mechanical system that operated similarly to

that of a fill tank. Waves were generated by three electric turbo pumps with 600 total horsepower rather than air pressure. The eight fill tanks or chambers were located behind the deepest section of the pool which was eight feet in depth. When the water surface reached a set level, a wall opened up allowing water to rush out the bottom. The first wave generated for the new attraction during testing was a marvel in itself. The waves were so powerful that they went to the end of the pool, continued onto the midway and washed the newly installed landscaping, sod and lounge chairs into the lake. Adjustments to the operating system were made and proved to be a success in that they did not exceed the edge of the pool as it did on the first trial run. During testing of The Wave, Sea World became suspicious that the park officials could not control the waves strength and contacted a local news station to visit Geauga Lake. By the time of the news station visit, the park had The Wave operational, and the park received a lot of positive public relations from the visit.

In typical Geauga Lake fashion, moving attractions in the park had become common practice, thus both the Trabant and Tilt-a-Whirl were relocated next to the Corkscrew to make room for the new wave pool attraction. About half of the dirt and soil excavated during the construction process was moved on two sides of the midway creating mounds and about 30 trees and 1,500 shrubs planted. In the center of the midway were planters installed using formerly used railroad ties. The Wave was an instant hit with guests and helped bolster attendance to just shy of 1 million visitors. When the advertising campaign for The Wave was unveiled to the public, excitement grew as the campaign never revealed what The Wave was, further establishing the marketing genius of Geauga Lake's management team. The advertising campaign was extremely exciting, and the logo was equally engaging. The tsunami-like waves were a guest favorite, especially for those who waited for the intervals on rafts, when a horn sounded, warning guests the next waves were about to begin.

Season passes to Geauga Lake cost $34.95 in 1984. At that time, only paddle boats on the lake and miniature golf cost an extra charge. Discounted day tickets could be purchased at Fazio Supermarkets for $24.25 and regular admission was $10.95. Like past seasons, children under three years of age were admitted free to the park and senior citizens, 60 years and older, could enter the park for only $6.95. Parking was $1 for a car, $2 for recreational vehicles, and buses were free.

While 1984 was a wildly successful season for Geauga Lake with attendance up 5% and revenue up 8.3% to $14.2 million, it was a somber year for nearby Idora Park in Youngstown. The park lost two of its most popular attractions, one of which was the Wildcat roller coaster in a devastating fire leading up to opening day. The park, which had been up for sale for a number of years, closed at the end of the summer forever. Loyal guests of Idora Park were upset at the decision, but with Geauga Lake and nearby Kennywood in Pittsburgh adding multi-million-dollar attractions almost yearly, the inevitable had arrived. The market shifted again and this time heavily favored both Geauga Lake and Kennywood. While Kennywood picked up some of Idora's group business events, Geauga Lake hired Idora's sales managers.

Funtime Guaranteed

Elsewhere, Funtime Inc. entered into an agreement with the City of Columbus and the Ohio Company (who originally established the Columbus Zoo) to operate Goodings Zoo Park for the Gooding Family who looked to retire. Rechristened as Wyandot Lake Adventure Park, the newly renamed and designed family amusement park opened on May 24, 1984. The redesigned park was designed by Rolf Roth, then an architectural leader in the amusement industry. Funtime went to work immediately and, similar to Geauga Lake, installed a new wave pool and made general improvements to the amusement park area. The new waterpark section to the old amusement park was located across the street from the main entrance to the zoo. Over the next decade, Funtime Inc. invested $4 million toward improving Wyandot Lake. The Funtime formula and industry leading efforts of integrating the traditional amusement park and waterpark into one facility proved successful at all three Funtime properties.

The park originated as a small recreational picnic and recreational spot in 1896. The Gooding Family, who purchased the property in the 1940s to store traveling amusement park equipment, decided to set up equipment in hopes to establish a formal park in 1956. That year, Goodings Zoo Park opened the Sea Dragon roller coaster. The park featured many traditional family and popular children's attractions, and for Funtime, operating the park offered exposure for the company to encourage visitors in Columbus to travel to Geauga Lake. Operating Wyandot Lake also offered the company the opportunity to remove rides from Geauga Lake and relocate them to Columbus. A perfect example was with the Rock-O-Plane being relocated to Wyandot Lake in 1984. Years later, other former Geauga Lake rides would make the move as well.

Regarding the first season of operation at Wyandot, Van Voorhis commented in a November 24, 1984, *Amusement Business* article:

> "Wyandot Lake, in its first year of operation, had an excellent season with attendance just shy of 300,000 and with revenue of $2.7 million."

Over at sister park Darien Lake, attendance increased 200,000 visitors over 1983, making for record attendance in 1984. The decision to develop Darien Lake into a complete family entertainment complex was a wise decision. In early 1985, the Ohio Company, already owners of 28% of Funtime, purchased an additional amount of preferred stock at $5 per share giving them a controlling 52% controlling interest in Funtime, Inc. Because of past success and future potential the Ohio Company saw in its investment, Funtime Inc. announced on February 8, 1985 they acquired the remaining 50% ownership in the Darien Lake partnership from Paul Snyder. Combined attendance at all three parks totaled 2,645,800 visitors. In a 1985 *Amusement Business* article, Van Voorhis said,

> *"We have a master plan which will develop Geauga Lake the way we want it over the next eight to 10 years." The plans call for moving the park's main entrance across the street, better utilization of the lake, relocating Kiddieland, widening the midways, improving landscaping and adding a major attraction every other year."*

Moving into the 1985 season, Funtime spent $1.8 million at Geauga Lake adding new food service and revenue facilities to the park. New were the full-service,

air-conditioned Funtime Sail Company, two piers with shops, a seafood bar, three new restrooms and expanded parking areas. The older Spaghetti House was razed to accommodate new landscaping surrounding the new Funtime Sail Company restaurant. The final addition was a lighthouse with two levels, with the lower level featuring a refreshment stand accessible to guests in The Wave. No new ride attractions were added in 1985, but the new additions to the park continued the company's plan to improve the facility at large and make enhancements yearly. The goal was to improve the overall guest experience no matter the age or interests.

After the company grew to own multiple parks, the ownership and management team of every property had a two-day retreat in October or November at the end of the park season. The retreat offered the teams time to meet and discuss plans for the upcoming season as well as management development opportunities. During this time, Funtime had built and developed a strong leadership team. The success of Funtime Incorporated caught the attention of industry leaders, including that of Harcourt Brace Jovanovich (HBJ), a book publishing company that purchased the Sea World parks in 1976.

A tentative agreement was announced that HBJ would purchase Geauga Lake for $23.1 million in a stock deal. The agreement called for Funtime to dispose of its interests at Darien Lake and Wyandot Lake. While HBJ approached Funtime Inc. about combining their operations and merging both Geauga Lake and Sea World into one park, the deal was ultimately terminated in early 1986 because Funtime Inc. was not interested in selling its Darien Lake or Wyandot Lake operations. HBJ was only interested in Geauga Lake and no other assets or liabilities. Because of that, the sale fell through.

Also in early 1986, Jim Meikle was named vice president and general manager of Geauga Lake. Prior to this appointment, Meikle oversaw the three-year, two-phase successful development of Boardwalk Shores. Geauga Lake and Funtime had proven themselves to be respectful owners and operators of amusement parks, and with their proven success, it was only a matter of time before additional offers from other buyers would arise. And while HBJ hoped to reapproach Funtime with a new offer, they eventually sold their amusement and marine park business to Anheuser Busch Company in 1989.

Like the prior year, 1986 saw steady improvements to the Geauga Lake experience, this time with Funtime spending a half million dollars renovating and redesigning the park's former Kiddieland into a new themed area called Rainbow Island. New rides included the Critter Express and a miniature log flume, while renamed and refurbished older rides included Salt Water Tugs, Lickety Split, Gumdrop Express, Smackers, Toot 'N' Hoots, Flying Jumbos, Space Patrol, and Rainbow Racers. In a May 22, 1986, *Akron Beacon Journal* article, Meikle commented:

> *"To remain competitive in our industry, we realize the need to add new attractions and to enhance the existing facilities for our guests. In addition to completely refurbishing each ride, we have added new rides and softened the entire area with creative landscaping."*

The park returned to the services of Rolf Roth who designed the new Rainbow Island. In addition to the rides, extensive landscaping with wishing wells were installed, shaded seating areas, benches with a new refreshment stand featuring soft drinks, hot dogs, hamburgers, and other snacks. Elsewhere, the park saw improvements to their picnic pavilion area and created a combination retail shop and original Cookie Company store. The Carousel was also restored, showing the park wished to retain the appeal of the past while looking toward the future. Rainbow Island became a land of memories, as the new themed area returned guests to a time of innocence when all was a simple adventure. Geauga Lake always catered to the families, and the charm and character of the park continued to attract loyal guests. Rainbow Island was not a first for the industry, but helped kickstart another industry first the following year.

Moving into 1987 and preparing to hire 1,500 seasonal employees, the park released an upbeat press release saying; "Fill your summer of '87 with sunshine, fresh air, new friends and a paycheck by becoming a part of the growing team of top-notch employees at Geauga Lake." In its television advertisements, the park advertised: 'This summer, the race is on." The new main attraction that summer was the Euroracers Grand Prix Raceway. Located next to the Corkscrew and along Route 43, the new upcharge attraction was not included in the pay-one-price admission but proved to be an immediate hit with guests. The new go-kart track featured 30 Formula K go-karts on a 1,500-foot course at speeds up to 12 miles per hour. For guests who chose not to ride, a small grandstand was constructed to view the track and races. While some doubted why a paying guest would pay extra for an attraction not included in the POP admission gate ticket, the Euroracer Grand Prix Raceway was so much of a success, it paid itself off in one year of operation. The uniqueness of the attraction extended to its sponsorship by ProCare, a division of Sohio. Employees working at the new Euroracer Grand Prix Raceway also wore ProCare uniforms.

Other changes in the park included the relocation of the Tilt-a-Whirl to the former site of the Calypso, the Trabant being moved to the former Ferris Wheel site, and the Flying Scooters finding a new home in Western Village. In keeping with the theme of families and attractions for everyone, live shows that season included the musical show "That's Entertainment" and a retrospective show called "The Heart of Rock N Roll." Additional entertainment in the park included a magic show, a mime, and an adventure film titled "Galaxy of Thrills" shown at the Cinema 180 theater. The park also unveiled in the middle of the season the new Stingray triple lane waterslide featuring a double speed slide and a 70-foot freefall slide. The death-defying slide was only for the bravest of riders who were instructed to lie down on their backs while crossing arms over the chest before going down the steep slide. With nothing holding a person in the slide other than gravity and the side of the slides, Stingray's popularity was proven by the long lines of riders waiting to test their courage. The freefall experience was so exhilarating at times, one may say it felt as if you were just falling through the air.

The year 1987 also marked a major change for parent company, Funtime Incorporated, as a group of executives led by Van Voorhis, Gasper Lococo and the Ohio Company leveraged a $63 million buyout of the company. Each stockholder received $7 per share of Funtime common stock, and the company became privately owned. The deal was completed on New Year's Eve of that year.

100 Years of Fun

The following season (1988) became a marketing year for the park when it opened on May 7. After years of never mentioning the park's origins or an official year of establishment as a recreational venue, Geauga Lake announced plans to celebrate its 100th anniversary that summer season. Not many parks had reached that milestone other than Cedar Point, Lake Compounce, and Rocky Point Park. In 1985, when the park closed the Big Ditch boat ride, park executives stated that the area would be developed for park expansion, including new attractions. The park even shared that phase one of the expanded area would feature a new roller coaster.

> *"Its energy relentless, its witness, unchallenged, its time forgotten, but now the legend or terror returns. The new Raging Wolf Bobs at Geauga Lake."*
>
> —*1988 Raging Wolf Bobs TV Commercial*

The $2.5 million Raging Wolf Bobs unveiled on Memorial Day Weekend in 1988 was inspired and styled after the legendary Bobs roller coaster at the now-closed Riverview Park in Chicago, Illinois. The new roller coaster was a collaboration between the Dinn Corporation and Curtis D Summers Inc. Charles Dinn, who previously worked at Kings Island, was at that time the leading expert in roller coaster construction. Summers, an engineer by trade, worked with Dinn on numerous projects and other ride-related projects in the industry. Ride vehicles for the new attraction were provided by the Philadelphia Toboggan Company. The new Raging Wolf Bobs featured a similar layout to the original ride in Chicago but with modified hills and profile. Original blueprints from the Bobs

Jim Meikle (top) and Jeff Lococo (bottom) played vital roles in the success of the park.

roller coaster were provided to Geauga Lake by the National Amusement Park Historical Association. The new roller coaster, soon to be the largest ride of its kind at Geauga Lake, was eagerly anticipated by guests. The roller coaster was 79 feet tall featuring 3,426 feet of track and multiple large, banked turns throughout its layout.

The ride's inspiration came from Jeff Lococo. During Lococo's time at Great America in Chicago, he heard many stories about Riverview Park and its infamous Bobs roller coaster. Knowing the marketing potential and after conducting research, it was determined a new wooden roller coaster would be a great addition to the park. The opening of the ride helped attract over 1 million visitors to the park for its 100th anniversary season celebration. A new midway was constructed to the ride, further developing and expanding the park's footprint. Not only did the addition of Raging Wolf Bobs add a new roller coaster to the park's lineup, its location allowed the opportunity for future additions to the park past Western Village. Attendance that year increased nearly 5% totaling 1.15 million visitors compared to the 1.10 million visitors from 1987. According to Vice President and General Manager Jim Meikle, attendance steadily increased 46% from 1982 when the park attracted 785,000 visitors. The continuous growth and success of Geauga Lake now made it the 33rd largest amusement park in the country by attendance. The addition of new attractions helped drive attendance, but in the long run, it was ownership's dedication to marketing the park to families, maintaining a successful business model, and operational plan.

Continued enhancements to the park consisted of the opening of the Mississippi River boat for lake cruises, the opening of the Waterfront Deck in Boardwalk Shores and a special events area and stage being relocated to a new area opposite

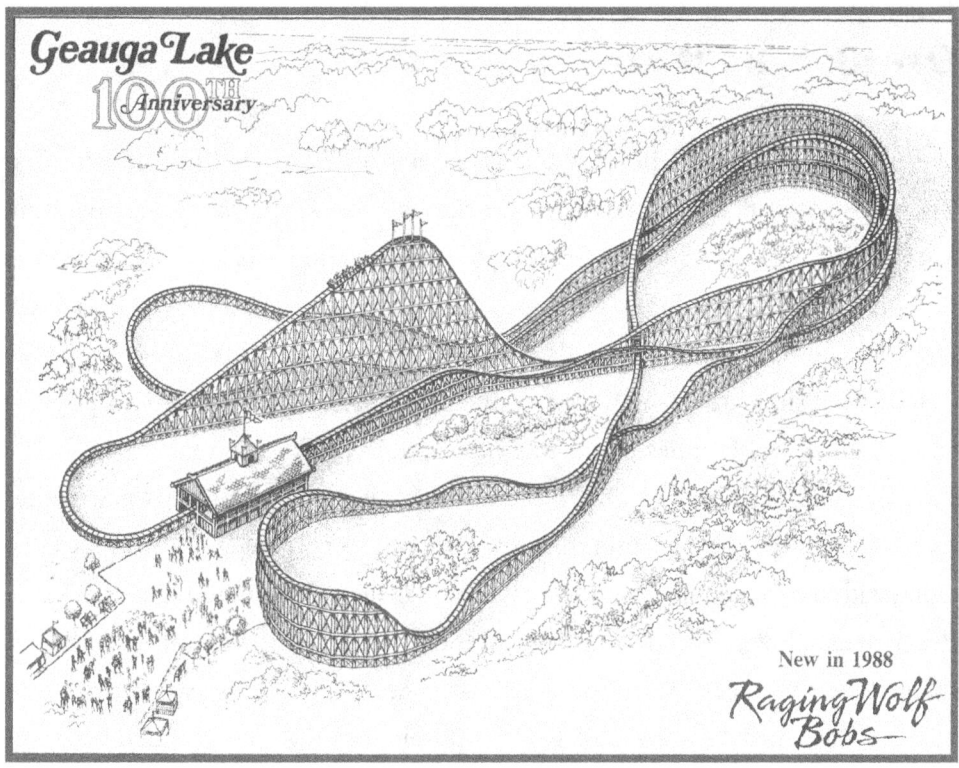

Raging Wolf Bobs. The park also renamed the Eastern Resorts Theater to the Palace Theater and Garrity's Fudge became Garrahy's Fudge Kitchen. Interestingly enough, the Garrahy's Fudge Kitchen name lasted one year as in 1989 it was renamed Collins Swiss Fudge. While the park celebrated its 100th anniversary season with much fanfare, the park also made a decision based on a growing trend at the time. American hand-carved carousels had become extremely valuable, and many parks across the country began selling off the rides entirely or selling individual horses because of their value. While an asking price of $900,000 was set, no one made an offer for the park's Carousel. Two years later, the park purchased a pipe organ with wooden pipes and a trio of snare, bass and timpani drums. The ride's original organ was destroyed in a 1952 fire, and the new organ brought back the magic and magnificent sound of days gone by. As the park closed for the season on September 25, it marked the final year for the Trabant, Patio Barbeque, Nautical Bar, and Kiddie Pool. While the Kiddie Pool was removed, it did not mean the park was forgetting about its youngest waterpark visitors.

Overflowing With Fun

Unveiled in 1989, Turtle Beach was a waterpark for children. This industry first was capped off with attractions such as Tortuous Tube, Turtle Chute, Snapper Run, Kahuna Kurls, Sneaky Squirts, Crayon Fountains, a children's lazy river, Hightide Fun Hats, Otter Wide Slide, Turtle Chase Run, Monkey Swing, Lily Pad Walk Log Roll and tumbling water walls. The new Turtle Beach also helped introduce Butch Hightide to the Fun Bunch characters. Turtle Beach proved so popular with children and families that it was expanded the following year in 1990. Turtle Beach and the Butch Hightide character were conceptualized by none other than Jeff Lococo. The $1.1 million expansion in 1990 included a "dry" play area, along with new water attractions. An additional 1.4 acres was added to the Turtle Beach area, allowing children to control their play activities and provide a more interactive experience. Turtle Beach, situated next to Rainbow Island, proved to be a one-stop area dedicated solely for children, and together spanned a total of 3.5 acres. New in 1990 were 26 palm trees imported from Florida to provide shade and a "Totally Rad" experience for the home of Butch Hightide. Butch Hightide was used frequently in the park's marketing campaigns from television, radio, and print media.

Aerial photo of the expanded Turtle Beach

With the expansion and increased promotion of Turtle Beach, the park opted to have Kool-Aid sponsor the area, similar to what it had done for other park attractions. During the offseason, the palm trees and tropical foliage seen at Turtle Beach were stored in the park's greenhouse. Innovative decision-making was the park's strength, and it was revealed through marketing research that it was desired by the individuals patronizing Geauga Lake. This long-term strategy led to many loyal and repeat visitors, which drove business and profit. In knowing this, the park sought to retain this patronage because management knew if they lost the regional market, they'd lose public interest. The key to any amusement park operating in the 1990s was to blend the best of the old and new attractions while keeping true to the park's identity. This was no easy task, but Geauga Lake seemed to have mastered this practice over the past two decades.

With the welcomed new additions to the park, the group sales business remained stronger than ever with 54% of the park's annual attendance coming from pre-paid tickets from group outings. With picnic groves able to accommodate 10,000 guests and plenty of space for group activities, management wanted to make sure a day of fun could be had by everyone. The group sales team worked diligently to personalize each outing at the park by customizing admission tickets, promotional materials, event equipment, and special appearances from Geauga Dog and the rest of the Fun Bunch. Welcoming businesses and organizations to the park was also key as proper signage was always displayed on a specific group's day for an outing at Geauga Lake. Large companies and organizations who held annual outings at the park included Eastern Ohio Gas, General Electric, Chrysler, Lubrizol, Lincoln Electric, Cleveland Electric, U.A.W. Local 122, University Hospitals of Cleveland, Babcock and Wilcox, Cleveland Pneumatic, and First National Bank. Geauga Lake aimed to offer competitive yet affordable pricing to all groups and individuals looking for a fun time at the park.

Park officials looked forward to welcoming return visitors, striving to keep the park fresh and appear new each season, even if that meant providing structures with a coat of fresh paint. Even the small details were cared for, such as signage, buildings, and names of revenue-generating areas such as food, games, and retail locations. Food stands such as Nature's Harvest were renamed Old Fashion Ice Cream, with Pizza and Cream renamed Midway Pizza. While some of the menu options for guests were updated yearly, the stands' food options remained mostly the same except for the name itself. Even the change of a name sparked interest from the paying guests and pushed them to think something new and exciting was added. By the 1990s, admission to the park was $13.50 with reduced admission of $8.50 after 5 p.m. Monday through Friday. Senior admission remained at $8.50 with children under 3, free. Parking fees were set at $3 a vehicle.

In the meantime, the parent company strategically added attractions to Darien Lake, which included a new children's themed area, a river raft ride called Grizzly Run and a new roller coaster, the Predator in 1990, which was built owing to the success of Raging Wolf Bobs at Geauga Lake. About $1.6 million was invested into Geauga Lake for 1991 in the form of two rides: the Mirage, a flying carpet ride, and the Casino, a Trabant ride themed to a roulette wheel. The new attractions were installed on an expanded midway dubbed the Lakeside Midway. Moved to that area of the park to accompany the new additions was the Spider, which sat in front of the Mirage and Casino. The Mirage was purchased from the closing Boardwalk and Baseball theme park in Florida, owned and operated by HBJ. In 1989, HBJ announced plans to sell some of its theme parks, which included Sea World Ohio, which it had owned since 1976. The addition of the Mirage and Casino extended the midway on the opposite side of the Big Dipper with mechanical rides and helped complete development of the property around the far turn of the coaster. What had been a quiet and dark area of the park after the water attractions of Boardwalk Shores closed for the evening, was now fully illuminated with lights, action, and screams.

To prepare for future additions, the Sky Glide, a sky ride located behind The Wave, was retired in 1993. While the early 1990s' economic downturn put a halt to some future plans, the park did install the Texas Twister at a cost of $1.8 million. Designed and manufactured by German ride manufacturer Huss, the Top Spin, which is the generic name for the ride, lifts 40 riders to a height of 60 feet in a vehicle that rocks back and forth and flips upside down. While the ride did not appeal to all guests, it was an extremely visually appealing ride. The heavily themed Texas Twister was also the first of its kind in the United States. The park invested another $300,000 into the ride's theme, creating what looked to be an Old Western town destroyed by a twister or tornado. All of the ride's theming was designed and created in-house by the park's team. The Texas Twister was not only a unique product, but it was an attraction that did not put Geauga Lake in competition with any other park in the market. Management did not want to compete directly with regional amusement parks by having similar attractions. After all, the variety of family and thrill rides is what created the charm of Geauga Lake under Funtime ownership.

Other than the new ride, the park focused its efforts on maintaining the park's current infrastructure and landscape. Other major projects included the completion of a five-year rebuild project on Big Dipper, which included every piece of wood and hardware being replaced. Additionally, the park carefully restored and refurbished the Carousel. With plans in place to install a new outdoor theater, the park closed the Gold Rush Theater and converted the space into an arcade. The new outdoor Stage Coach Theater was built to accommodate shows and events for 3,000 guests. The new theater replaced an older stage that could only accommodate 400 guests. Additionally, new benches were purchased and installed throughout the entire park and much effort was put into improving the overall image of the park. As was customary every season, especially due to the economic downturn, landscaping throughout the park was significantly enhanced, as well as general park painting and board replacement at the Boardwalk Shores area.

The economic downturn proved too much for an investment into a new ride until at least the 1995 season. The Miniature Golf Course, which had remained popular for several years, was quietly retired and replaced with a new attraction called Butch Hightides Funtime Fortress designed by Little Tykes. Even though the park slowed its continued re-investment projects, the park still catered to families and was considered to be a great value. Geauga Lake was seen as an upgrade to most regional amusement parks, not only because of its attractions but because of the cleanliness and general appearance of the facility. With Sea World as its neighbor, even during economic downturns, the two parks remained a smart destination for families, especially those looking to travel from out of state for mini vacations.

Under the ownership of Funtime Inc., Geauga Lake continued its steady group sales business with pre-booked outings. The largest-capacity single day ever held at the park during the Funtime era was 31,000 guests. The steady cashflow proved that even during difficult years, avoiding financial difficulty was possible. And it surely seemed impossible Geauga Lake would ever run into financial difficulty due to the years of success and strong relationship it had built with the local community.

In late 1992, Funtime looked to grow its park portfolio again. This time they were tapped to manage and turnaround a struggling amusement park in Bristol, Connecticut, called Lake Compounce. This opportunity allowed Funtime to not only manage another park, but the potential to eventually own a third amusement park — more importantly, the oldest operating amusement park in the country. Challenges existed in the new partnership, including many back taxes, but eventually a three-year $35 million revitalization plan was announced. Following a similar business plan seen at Wyandot Lake and Darien Lake, a new waterpark was planned for 1996 followed by new rides in subsequent seasons. As for Geauga Lake, Gasper Lococo envisioned the park becoming more of a destination point with a campground and hotel. By late 1994, Funtime signed a management agreement to operate Lake Compounce. Funtime Inc. did not want to be acquired by a larger company, and one of the ways ownership sought to avoid this was to manage or acquire additional amusement parks. One way or the other, it was only a matter of time before Geauga Lake became part of a larger company that owned and managed multiple amusement parks.

The Big Dipper offered thrills for generations of families and for many, their first roller coaster ride. At one time, picnic tables could be found and used within the grassy area inside the rides turnaround.

Gold Rush

Merry Oldies

The Carousel as seen during the 1980s.

Geauga Lake enthusiastically embraced a variety of live entertainment to its daily operations. Each season, the park featured indoor and outdoor forms of entertainment. Indoor entertainment allowed guests an opportunity to sit down and escape the outdoor elements.

Construction for the Boardwalk Shores Neptune's Falls waterslide was well underway when this 1983 photo was taken.

The Undertow

Stingray waterslides

Landing pool for the Neptune's Falls

This 1991 photo shows The Wave and lake from the Skyscraper

The new Boardwalk Shores featured attractions for adults, families, and children. In addition to the water attractions, this area of the park featured a wide range of foot treats including beer and wine.

The addition of Turtle Beach exceeded expectations and offered parents and guardians more opportunities to interact with their children. The area was designed to promote physical, imaginative and creative play. Butch Hightide, a new mascot introduced for Turtle Beach was featured throughout Turtle Beach, on souvenirs, and in various park advertisements.

Mike Funyak

Geauga Lake

Mike Funyak

Geauga Lake

CHAPTER 5

An American Classic
1995-1999

In August 1995, Premier Parks purchased Funtime Inc for $60 million. The deal was announced the month prior with a letter of intent for the purchase being signed on June 16. The shocking news sent waves through the amusement industry as the new owners had only entered the amusement industry 13 years earlier. With the purchase of the Funtime Group, Premier Parks bought a company that was already larger than itself. Prior to the purchase, Premier Parks consisted of two parks, Frontier City in Oklahoma City and Adventure World between Washington, D.C. and Baltimore, Maryland. Geauga Lake originally wanted to install a 183-foot tall Skycoaster attraction for the 1995 season, but Bainbridge Township would not issue a permit for the attraction because of a height restriction. There was talk of the park being for sale, but Funtime ownership insisted they did not want to be purchased by a large conglomerate. In April 1994, management changes occurred at Funtime with Chief Operating Officer

Bruce Walborn replacing Dale Van Voorhis as president and CEO. The other three top managers moved up the corporate ladder and Geauga Lake received a new logo. In January 1995, James Bouy was named vice president and general manager of Geauga Lake, returning to the company after serving as general manager at Kennywood Park. Previously, Buoy was vice president and general manager of Darien Lake before moving into his role at Kennywood Park earlier in the decade. Changes were in the air, especially after Premier Parks purchased the Funtime parks. As the sale of Geauga Lake became official, it was announced the park would not close for the season in the fall as originally planned. 1995 became the first year a Halloween event called Hallowscream occurred at Geauga Lake and like Oktoberfest, proved to be a successful addition to the park's events and operating calendar. Shortly after the sale of Geauga Lake, it became known that the new ownership was determined to expand the park and one day purchase Sea World across the lake.

Premier Parks, originally known as Tierco Group, was a real estate company and entered the amusement industry when it purchased Frontier City in Oklahoma City, Oklahoma. The company was run by Chairman and Chief Executive Officer Kieran Burke whose background was in law and as an investment banker.

President and Chief Operating Officer Gary Story started working in the amusement industry as a teenager, rose through the ranks and had recently been the general manager at Frontier City for five years prior to the acquisition of Geauga Lake. In purchasing Funtime Inc., Premier Parks also acquired the management agreement of the oldest operating amusement park in the United States, Lake Compounce in Connecticut. Kennywood Park Corporation, which owned three parks in Pennsylvania, including Kennywood near Pittsburgh, also explored the possibility of purchasing Funtime Incorporated. The Kennywood group established plans to not only purchase Funtime but move members of its management team to oversee the newly acquired parks. At the last minute, Premier Parks entered the picture and offered significantly more than the Kennywood group. Since late 1994, Premier Parks was aggressively looking to buy parks that could attract between 350,000 to 1.5 million visitors each year. For both companies, not only was the portfolio of the company attractive, but the existing management team was also just as important. Although the Kennywood Park Corporation was outbid, they were ready to be competitive with the new owners of Geauga Lake. Not only was the purchasing of a regional amusement park occurring in Ohio, family-owned parks of all sizes were being purchased across the country.

Elsewhere, Premier Parks remained on a buying spree and purchased other amusement parks such as Elitch Gardens in Denver, Colorado, and The Great Escape in Queensbury, New York. During this time, Premier Parks invested in waterparks at Darien Lake, Elitch Gardens, and The Great Escape. Originally, Premier Parks, most notably COO Gary Story, envisioned building a new amusement park from the ground up in the New England area. The New England states were once a hotbed for amusement parks, however, beginning in the late 1980s, many of the smaller independently owned amusement parks closed. This was in large part due to a lack of owner succession planning, increased insurance and operating expenses, and tough competition from investment companies and corporations entering the amusement industry. These outside companies were able to invest millions of dollars into their properties and obtain buying power for not just general park inventory such as food supplies and game plush, but also from ride manufacturers and suppliers. Shortly after the purchase of Funtime Incorporated, Premier Parks determined they would terminate the management deal at Lake Compounce to focus efforts elsewhere. When Premier Parks became a public company in 1996, it raised nearly $70 million. This money was used to purchase additional amusement parks and invest heavily in the company's portfolio of parks.

The Kennywood Park Corporation re-entered the picture and saw the potential to take over ownership of Lake Compounce. Considered respected leaders within the industry, the Kennywood Park Corporation now reorganized as Kennywood Entertainment, paid off the park's debt and capitalized on state funds to revitalize Lake Compounce over multiple years. Considered one of the greatest stories in the amusement park industry, the Kennywood group tapped industry leaders and members of its existing team to turn Lake Compounce into the premier family amusement park in the region. The New England amusement park scene had changed significantly in the past decade. Many of the parks in the area closed or struggled financially, some even filed for bankruptcy. At the time of purchasing Funtime, Premier Parks also looked into the possibility of taking over operation of Rocky Point Park, but with an estimated $40 million investment of renovating the park, ongoing legal action, and the possibility of a new theme park being built, plans for Rocky Point Park were abandoned.

Another amusement park operator, Six Flags Theme Parks, reached a preliminary agreement with Mashantucket Pequot Indians, owners of the Foxwoods Casino, to build a 200-acre theme park on land owned by the tribe. For Gary Story, the closing of Rocky Point provided an opportunity to purchase used rides for parks in the Premier Park portfolio. Story, who originally started in park operations at Six Flags Over Mid-America, had a fondness for older attractions. In the amusement industry, each seasoned professional has a passion for one specific area, and for Story it was mechanical rides and maintaining older industry attractions. And while rides were purchased from the closing Rocky Point Park, the new large Foxwoods theme park was never built. Premier Parks jumped at a new opportunity in New England when they purchased Riverside Park in Agawam, Massachusetts, in late 1996 from the Carroll Family. With Premier Parks entering the New England market, dreams of building and/or acquiring their own park came to fruition. Over the next several years, Premier Parks would transform Riverside Park into a new experience for guests. Many of the older attractions were removed to make way for new roller coasters, other rides, and a new waterpark. Not only did the park start to see an infusion of capital dollars, but the entire park was also redesigned.

Adding New Ingredients

Entering its first year of full ownership at Geauga Lake, Premier Parks announced its commitment to operate each of the properties as individual parks because each local destination was a niche market. Plans for Geauga Lake included creating two new themed areas; a 1950s theme and an early American theme. According to Gary Story, the incorporation of themed concepts at Geauga Lake was part of

Corkscrew removal

a two-year, $20 million plan for the company's six parks. Additionally, Story announced the main entrance plaza and gate at Geauga Lake would receive a makeover with a new ornate, traditional American look further establishing the classic feel of an amusement park. The renovations to the main entrance area included expanded ticket and guest relation offices. The family-oriented atmosphere was further emphasized with the park's new logo and tagline "An American Classic."

Other noticeable changes occurred when travelers witnessed the dismantling of the Corkscrew roller coaster and Rocket Ships. Replacing the Corkscrew and Rocket Ships would be a Vekoma Boomerang roller coaster called Mind Eraser. Manufactured in the Netherlands and shipped from overseas, Mind Eraser took riders forward and then backward along the same track. The new roller coaster stood at 124 feet tall and traveled through its boomerang and looping course at a speed of 45 miles per hour. Elsewhere in the park, Grizzly Run opened next to Raging Wolf Bobs in an area originally supposed to be home to a Skycoaster attraction. Grizzly Run, a white-water themed raft ride that proved popular at Darien Lake under the Funtime era, had its name used again for the

Grizzly Run

installation at Geauga Lake. Similar to the attraction at Darien Lake, ride manufacturer Intamin, also designed the ride for Geauga Lake.

Other noticeable changes occurring in 1996 were the renaming of park attractions: the Enterprise became known as Silver Bullet, Gold Rush was renamed Cuyahoga River Logging Company, and the Euroracers Granprix was renamed Thunder Alley Speedway. While these name changes seemed subtle and somewhat unnecessary, it may have also been a precursor of what was ahead. That summer also marked the 70th birthday for the Big Dipper, which was fitting since it was also the International Year of the Roller Coaster. By the end of the operating season, Premier Parks was the seventh largest amusement park company in the United States measured by annual attendance. While it was two spots ahead of Cedar Fair, the owners of Cedar Point, Cedar Fair, brought in more revenue and Cedar Point alone attracted 2.3 million more visitors than Geauga Lake. In a summer 1996 press release for the park, Director of Marketing John Collins said:

> "Being the only rollercoaster of its kind in the region, the Mind Eraser will give our guests a ride they will not soon forget. We are very excited to have two new attractions. The Mind Eraser alone is a fantastic addition, but to also offer Grizzly Run this season – it's icing on the cake."

While Geauga Lake and its sister parks continued to experience growth in attendance, none of the parks were designed to handle extremely large crowds. Like Geauga Lake, the other parks within the Premier Parks umbrella were not laid out in a similar manner to that of Cedar Point, Valleyfair, or Worlds of Fun. Parks such as Kings Island, Carowinds, and Six Flags Over Texas were designed specifically to accommodate millions of visitors each year and thousands of visitors daily. Parks like Geauga Lake developed with the ever-changing market. However, the source of the park's continued success was its group sales business and pre-sold tickets. Geauga Lake was starting to drift away from this traditional, yet-successful business model with the addition of new, major, non-family-friendly thrill rides. Behind the scenes, personnel changes took place with Jim Bouy moving to sister park Elitch Gardens as general manager and Jeff Lococo to general manager at Geauga Lake who previously served in the same role at Wyandot Lake.

For the second full year under Premier Parks' ownership, Geauga Lake saw the addition of Mr. Hyde's Nasty Fall and Hook's Lagoon, an interactive waterplay structure. Mr. Hyde's Nasty Fall was one of the attractions purchased at the Rocky Point Park auction the year prior and saw riders ascend a 125-foot structure before being moved horizontally. After being suspended for a few seconds, the

four-passenger ride vehicle entered an intense freefall and an ominous curve as riders then faced the sky on their backs. At the end of the brake, the ride vehicle would travel backward, reorienting riders to an upright position and returning them to the load and unload station. The cleverly named and themed attraction fit in nicely with the park's ride lineup and area of the park that turned into a 1950s themed area. While the ride was popular, it was already an older attraction, with a storied history, one of which involved an incident at its original location at Great America in Chicago, Illinois. To make room for Mr. Hyde's Nasty Fall, the Yo-Yo, Musik Express, and Tilt-a-Whirl were relocated in the park.

Hook's Lagoon

Hook's Lagoon, installed at the corner of the park by The Wave and lake, featured a towering five-story tree house and pirate ship. Accompanying the 17th century replica pirate ship were special effects and other interactive water features. At the top of the structure was a tipping bucket that once full of water would empty on top of guests below. Every five minutes, 1,000 gallons of water was poured over a series of platforms. A ship's bell sounded an alarm to warn guests of the potential drenching. The new interactive water activity structure was a welcome compliment to the already popular waterpark. Turtle Beach had proven so popular with families at Geauga Lake, Premier Parks decided to build similar children's family attractions and areas at both Darien Lake and Wyandot Lake. In a spring and summer 1997 press release, General Manager Jeff Lococo commented on the addition of Hook's Lagoon:

> *It's specifically designed to allow children to interact with their parents in an exciting and stimulating environment..... Equipped with dozens of hoses, funnels, tunnels, spouts and other water-spraying devices,*

> guests are sure to experience a unique water adventure with each visit to Hook's Lagoon."

Geauga Lake always considered itself an alternative option to Cedar Point, and former ownership also recognized Cedar Point as its greatest competition. This ideology was not necessarily due to the physical number of rides and attractions, but it was the operational practices and standards established at Cedar Point that made the park a highly respected facility within the industry. Other amusement park owners such as those who owned nearby Kennywood saw it the same way. If anything, parks such as Cedar Point and Kings Island made all other amusement park owners' better operators. If a park can't compete on the same level or number of attractions featured elsewhere, what it can do is focus on the entire guest experience provided by cleanliness, guest service, popular attractions and enjoyable food and games. Geauga Lake prided itself on the basics of family entertainment; however, slowly but surely the culture at the park was changing. Prior ownership never intended to compete directly with Cedar Point because they already had a proven audience and control of their market. Additionally, Cedar Point had little to no debt, Geauga Lake and even Funtime Incorporated did have debt to its name. Behind the scenes for park employees, continuous changes were abundant. Matters were to become even more interesting in February 1998, when Premier Parks Inc. announced it was purchasing Six Flags Theme Parks from Time Warner Inc. and Boston Ventures for $965 million, plus the assumption of $890 million in debt.

A New Direction

The deal to purchase Six Flags Theme Parks tripled Premier Park's revenue and shocked the amusement industry at large. From a 1998 *New York Times* article: "… It is a bit like a minor league team buying the New York Yankees." Six Flags' 1997 revenue was three times the amount Premier Parks earned in the same calendar year. The question remained, how would this deal affect the existing amusement parks owned by Premier Parks, and what was the future of Geauga Lake?

The answer was revealed when the park unveiled another major addition at a $10 million expense in the suspended looping roller coaster called Serial Thriller. The new roller coaster was built on the lakefront on property formerly occupied by the Big Ditch and anchored the newly themed Coyote Creek area, formerly known as Western Village. The new Serial Thriller featured 2,172 feet of track and a vertical loop of 90 feet. There were five inversions sending riders on a first-of-its-kind experience at the park. The park also opened its newly acquired 127-site campground, the Silverhorn Resort, adjacent to the park. In the spring, the park also purchased the 146-room Aurora Woodlands Inn located nearby. While the company continued its spending ways, the merger of Premier Park and Six Flags wasn't the easiest. In a November 2, 1998, *Amusement Business* article by Tim O'Brien, Gary Story discussed the different structures of the two companies and that few levels should exist between the top and those who deal with the public. CEO Burke even commented:

"The parks, not the corporate offices, need to drive the business."

Serial Thriller opened in 1998 on the location that was once occupied by the Sky Glide and Big Ditch. Construction proved difficult especially with the pouring of concrete for the rides footers into the lake.

As with any company merger or buyout, impending changes do occur, and some existing employees become unhappy with the new direction of the company. The ongoing purchases and heavy investment into Geauga Lake brought not only an increase of annual attendance but an increase in traffic on the roadways upsetting local residents, including local government officials. Since the very beginning of the park, the roadways to the park experienced increased traffic. The layout of the neighboring community hindered the expansion of the roadways, especially the development of additional lanes. But after all, Geauga Lake was a regional amusement park, not aimed at being a destination park for travelers from all over the country. Traffic congestion on highway 43 and Ohio 306 became controversial, and local officials' opinion of the park began to change. New retail and housing in the surrounding community began to put a strain on the roadway's capacity, and Geauga Lake and Sea World were blamed by some locals for the continuous traffic jams. While the two parks continued to operate in unison, the region's development in conjunction with that of Geauga Lake all contributed to the ongoing traffic concerns coming in and out of Bainbridge Township and Aurora, Ohio. In a comment to *Amusement Business* in 1998, Premier Parks COO Gary Story said:

> *"We have carefully analyzed all our parks to see which ones would be good candidates for the Six Flags brand."*

Did the comment mean Geauga Lake would become a Six Flags park or feature characters from DC comics or the popular Warner Brothers Looney Tunes? If this occurred, would that mean even greater market appeal and an increase of motorized traffic to the area? For the immediate future, the public was left with questions, pondering what would happen to their beloved regional family amusement park or Sea World. $35 million was spent on park improvements in 1999, including two new attractions: the Giant Wheel and the Time Warp, which carried 48 riders in two vehicles about 50 feet in the air flipping them 360 degrees. The 110-foot Giant Wheel was installed at the end of the entrance midway next to the lake and became a centerpiece for the park. It featured 24 gondolas lifting riders 12 stories into the sky. The park also proposed and installed a new Skycoaster attraction called Geronimo. The attraction stood 100 feet high, but the local ordinance only allowed attractions to be 65 feet. The addition of the new Geronimo was not without controversy. Nearby residents were unhappy with the park's decision to build the attraction in a location near homes where the maximum permissible height was 65 feet. A decree, agreed to by the park in 1996 to settle lawsuits, allowed the park to ask the local zoning board for permission to exceed the restriction.

Time Warp as seen in its debut season

The additions of these tall and major attractions meant only one thing; major changes were on the horizon for the park. One way or the other, the new owners of Geauga Lake would do as they pleased. Another challenge due to the accelerated growth of the park was finding seasonal employees for the 1999 operating season. The addition of multiple attractions over the last four years required hiring of additional seasonal, part-time, and full-time employees. That year, Sea World received 20% fewer job applications than in previous years. To avoid hiring shortages, Geauga Lake increased its hourly rate for seasonal employees by 15 cents an hour to fill the open position needed in the food department. Between 1996 and 1999, Premier Parks invested an estimated $35 million into Geauga Lake. It was clear Premier Parks wanted to attract part of Cedar Point's market and compete directly with them.

Story commented to Tim O'Brien years prior in a November 1995 *Amusement Business* article about the importance of building a park's equity through its own identity. Story talked about the individuality of all properties Premier Parks owned, which he felt was important because of the parks being locally oriented. Story emphasized the importance of keeping the park regionalized and not wanting to compete with other larger parks. Fast forward three years later, it seemed Geauga Lake's future was no longer to be just a regional amusement park, but was being positioned to become a destination mega theme park.

Toward the end of the 1999 season, it was clear to the general public that major developments and changes were occurring for the 2000 season. Rainbow Island had quietly closed, and many of its rides relocated to an area by the main entrance in what looked to be a temporary setup. The park saw significant changes in previous years, yet those changes, called "improvements," might have been seen as changes for the sake of change. Even HalloScream saw change in 1999, with the event now being called Fright Fest. What was visible to guests at the end of the 1999 season was not what they became accustomed to. Attendance at the park was flat, and the integration of Premier Parks and Six Flags was fully underway. Several parks — Darien Lake, Elitch Gardens, Kentucky Kingdom, Marine World and Adventure World, all owned by the company were rebranded as Six Flags parks. The inevitable was bound to occur at Geauga Lake. As major project planning occurred in the days ahead, Jeff Lococo was named head of project development and Jake Bateman assumed the role of general manager.

On December 8, 1999, the news was made official: Geauga Lake was to be transformed into Six Flags Ohio. Chairman and CEO of Six Flags Kiernan Burke stated in a press conference that the investments made in Geauga Lake between 1996 to 1999 were leading up to the park being transformed into a mega theme park. With four new roller coasters, a new and improved waterpark, a new children's area, and other park projects underway, Six Flags touted Geauga Lake would be improved and make its mark on the regional theme park business.

While the change was said to be an improvement, it was a major transformation and overhaul to an existing amusement park. Many of the park's existing attractions were removed: The Wave, Casino, Flying Scooters, Scrambler, Mirage, Tilt-a-Whirl, and even the popular arcade. What was once a family-oriented, traditional amusement park with themed elements, along with a strong picnic business, was now going to compete directly with the likes of Cedar Point and Kings Island for the best thrill and destination park in Ohio. This new direction shifted the park away from the family atmosphere the park was renowned throughout the region. With over $40 million spent upgrading the park in one year, some speculated if the park could sustain such growth. The Funtime era had officially culminated, and in its place a new era rushed in.

Every summer guests of all ages enjoyed Paddle Boats and even more so, the Gold Rush ride as they traveled through splashing, refreshing water in an action packed log ride.

"Whatta the kids wanna be when they grow up? Maybe a pilot? A Sailor? A race car driver? Or even an explorer? Find out when you bring them to our Rainbow Island fantasy land."

—1989 PARK BROCHURE

Turtle Beach featured various pools, crayon fountains, tumbling water walls, and twisting dipping water slides, and towers.

Geauga Lake employed hundreds of seasonal workers each summer. For many workers, the park provided opportunities to develop work ethic, leadership skills and forge lasting friendships. For tenured workers, badges often mentioned their years of service.

Mike Funyak

The Euroracer was an industry first. In 1989, the parks Map and Information Guide said "Fasten your seatbelts and hold on tight, the race is on at the Euroracer Grand Prix Raceway as you maneuver the sleek Formula K Race Car through 1500 ft. of grueling twists and curves."

Mike Funyak

Geauga Lake

This season take a heart-stopping sky-dive on Geauga Lake's new Dual Skyswing, Geronimo"

-1999 Park Brochure

Mike Funyak

Geauga Lake

Mike Funyak

The lift hills of Mind Eraser carried riders backward before sending them through a cobra roll and along the track again in reverse. The ride was renamed Head Spin in 2004.

Mike Funyak

The Flying Scooter, a park staple since 1958 entertained riders through the 1999 season.

During the 1990s, Geauga Lake matured as a park featuring a mix of nostalgia, traditional family amusements and new modern thrills rides

In the latter half of the decade, the additions and changes to the park became more aggressive and frequent. These changes to the parks landscape and overall operations were only a sign of what was to come beginning in the new century.

CHAPTER 6

Six Flags 2000-2003

Twenty new attractions including four new roller coasters debuted when the park opened for the 2000 operating season. While some attractions were relocated, many others were removed along with some buildings. The $40 million investment included not just new attractions but enhanced retail shops, food stands and a new waterpark called Hurricane Harbor. Most of the retail and food locations throughout the park received new names or were expanded. New water attractions such as a brand new 25,000-square-foot relocated wave pool next to Route 43, and a new 1,000-foot lazy river were constructed.

Due to the location of the new wave pool, the renamed Bellaire Express monorail track had to be partially removed and rerouted to travel around the wave pool. The existing Turtle Beach and Hook's Lagoon attractions remained with new additions. Shipwreck Falls, a shoot-the-chutes attraction was installed next to the new lazy river and required the removal of the Mirage, Casino, and Black Widow and games building from 1925. The installation of Shipwreck Falls

demanded the removal of the park's former older arcade located across from Big Dipper. In place of The Wave, was Looney Tunes Boom Town, which featured seven new children's attractions, a foam factory, and a larger-than-life interactive play structure. The new complex featured various characters and themed elements from the Looney Tunes cartoons such as Bugs Bunny, Marvin the Martian, Tweetie Bird, Sylvester, and the Road Runner.

Construction contractors were brought in from all over the area to work on the various additions and projects underway at the park. The installation of four roller coasters alone moved the park into direct competition with Cedar Point, which by this time earned a reputation for its roller coasters. While the new Six Flags Ohio would open four new roller coasters, Cedar Point would unveil the $25 million Millennium Force previously announced in July 1999. Not only was the Millennium Force to be Cedar Point's new star roller coaster in 2000, it was also going to be the world's tallest and fastest roller coaster.

Four New Coasters

For the new Six Flags Ohio, the unique Superman Ultimate Escape featured 630 feet of a U-shaped track. The ride vehicle would launch out of the loading station into a spiraled track at 180 feet. The ride vehicle would then fall backward and

Superman Ultimate Escape under construction. Riders were seated two across in 14 rows for a total of 28 riders per rider cycle.

launch in reverse traveling up a straight spike. This was followed by two more launches before the ride ended. The ride was installed next to Route 43 and required the park to redesign the existing Go-Kart track, Thunder Alley Speedway. Superman Ultimate Escape utilized linear induction motors (LIMs), a newer technology at the time to produce the launches of 70 mph. It was the world's first vertical spiraling impulse roller coaster.

Bolliger & Mabillard (B&M), considered one of the top roller coaster designers of the 1990s, was contracted to design the park's new 161-foot-tall floorless roller coaster, Batman Knight Flight. The new 4,210-foot-long ride would be the world's longest floorless roller coaster and feature five inversions, including a 135-foot-tall loop, and a top speed of 65 mph. This ride was installed next to Serial Thriller on the front of the lake in a new area themed to Gotham City, which also featured the new Batman Stunt Show. The ride was also custom designed to fit the site in which it sat at the park and presented construction challenges not even seen during the construction of Serial Thriller.

To make room for the new roller coaster, the Yukon Yahoo was moved to the park's Coyote Creek area on the site formerly occupied by the Scrambler and Flying Scooters. Rethemed as Hay Bayler, a red barn was built around the ride to add to the theming. The Flying Scooter was retired and Scrambler was put in storage to undergo refurbishment for an upcoming season. Nearby, a family roller coaster, Road Runner Express, was installed behind the Dodgems, replacing three picnic pavilions. It was a Tivoli coaster from the German manufacturer Zierer. Another noticeable name change that season was Cuyahoga River Logging Company being renamed Deer Park Plunge.

The Villain, designed by Ohio-based Custom Coasters International was built next to the Double Loop and Geauga Lake Road and was considered a double-out-and-back ride. The Villain loading station and entrance was modeled to resemble that of the western area in which the ride was constructed. While The Villain was a wooden roller coaster, the track sat on a galvanized steel structure, which helped reduce maintenance costs. The ride's lift hill was 120 feet tall with the ride's top speed of 60 mph. The ride featured 12 drops, 14 turns, and a swooping turnaround that was featured twice during the ride cycle. The Double Loop, which previously featured a paint scheme with black track and supports, sported new colors for the 2000 season with a new mustard yellow colored track and purple supports. The addition of the Villain gave Six Flags Ohio the honor of being the only Six Flags theme park with three wooden roller coasters.

General admission for the 2000 season rose from $29 to $31 and an additional 1,200 parking spaces were added to the existing parking lot. Excitement was building for the park, and attendance was expected to be around 1.7 million visitors. While some welcomed the changes to the park, many saw the changes as a drastic departure from prior ownership's commitment to affordable family fun. In a new marketing campaign, guests could save up to $10 on a single general admission ticket with a specially marked Coca-Cola product can. Advertisements were also placed in Toys R Us locations near the aisles that featured toys from the DC Comic Series. In addition to the new Six Flags Ohio television commercials highlighting the four new roller coasters being installed, Hurricane Harbor had its own television advertisement in which it was said Six Flags Ohio now had a tropical paradise. Tourists and visitors from as far away as Illinois, Iowa, and Wisconsin were expected when the park reopened. The increase in park attendance also meant that local hotel and motel capacity could be pushed to capacity.

State and local officials agreed the new Six Flags Ohio would see an increase in summertime traffic on the nearby roadways leading to the park. Local community officials were concerned that the traffic congestion into Portage, Cuyahoga and Geauga County would be further compounded, especially on Route 43. Motorists were now going from a bad situation during the already busy summer months to a worse situation. To widen the highway, a plan would need to be developed and presented to the state Transportation Review Advisory Council. Previous attempts had been made to improve the roadways, but some locals objected due to it destroying the historical district between Aurora-Hudson Road and state Route 82. What was once a major issue for the park when Bill Kuhlman developed the property into a modern amusement park and entertainment facility in the 1920s, had peaked in full force. Further change occurred at the park when Jeff Lococo left his position at the park in March for a position with Great Wolf Lodge. Replacing him at the park was his cousin Augie Lococo who worked at the park for a number of years.

New Guide to Fun

The first season as Six Flags Ohio was deemed successful and plans for the 2001 season had already been put into place. In December 2000, land started to be cleared for the park's newest addition, a new flying roller coaster called X-Flight. The addition of X-Flight brought the park's total roller coaster count to ten. Riders turned upside down into a flying position and soared through 3,340 feet of track featuring eight inversions and speeds of 55 mph. Elsewhere, the park was

re-introducing the Mirage, now sporting a 1950s theme and renamed El Dorado. The El Dorado opened in a spot on the opposite side of Big Dipper. Additionally, The Black Widow was relocated to the park, now named Black Squid on the site formerly occupied by the Rotor, which was retired. Meanwhile Sea World's parent company, Busch Entertainment, sought to focus more on amusement rides and attractions at their various parks and not on the educational aspects. Busch Entertainment subsequently turned their attention toward offering to purchase the new Six Flags Ohio.

Then on January 10, 2001, only days after announcing X-Flight, Six Flags Inc. announced it reached an agreement with Busch Entertainment Corporation to purchase Sea World Ohio for $110 million. Plans called for the 232-acre marine

themed park to be combined with the adjacent 520 acre Six Flags Ohio, with Six Flags campgrounds and hotel properties to create a mega entertainment destination. The new mega park would be a total of 700 acres in size and the entire complex was renamed, Six Flags Worlds of Adventure. The agreement signed between both Six Flags and Sea World gave Six Flags ownership of the former Sea World but without the animals. The three killer whales had already been transported back to San Diego and the dolphins and emperor penguins would remain with Sea World. Six Flags Inc. then transferred dolphins from Six Flags Marine World in California to the new Wild Life section of Six Flags Worlds of Adventure to maintain the popular marine life shows.

The amusement rides on the opposite side of the lake would eventually adopt the Wild Rides name with the gates being called Wild Rides North Gate and the Wild Life South Gate. The park remained committed to an interactive dolphin show and sea lion show, but there was one show guests would truly miss, that which featured Shamu. While the popular Shamu show was gone, exhibits featuring penguins, sharks and walruses remained popular. Six Flags CEO and Chairman Kiernan Burke said that merging the two parks "provides an unbelievable opportunity for synergies and increased growth in attendance and revenue categories for Six Flags."

To help fill the space in the former Happy Harbor section of Sea World, flat rides were installed toward the end of the season which included Bounty, and the return of the Scrambler, now renamed Boardwalk Typhoon. Other new attractions consisted of a Turbo Bungy trampoline attraction which was an up-charge attraction not included in general addition and the Starcastle Voyage, which was added mid-season. While Six Flags did not acquire many of the marine animals, it did acquire two of Sea World's attractions: Mission: Bermuda Triangle and Pirates 4D Adventure. Elsewhere in the newly expanded footprint of the park, management moved the Batman Stunt Show to the now former Sea World Stadium and debuted the Batman Water Stunt Spectacular.

The attraction for out-of-towners visiting two drastically different parks in close proximity was gone. The competitive nature of the amusement park industry greatly changed in the 1990s and for many, the now $37 admission fee was steep. Merging the two facilities presented many changes, with one main factor

being how to solve the issue of connecting both sides of the lake into one cohesive facility. For years, the northwestern part of the lake next to Route 43 hosted cottages and houses while the other side of the lake behind Raging Wolf Bobs was primarily protected wetlands and undevelopable. While a ferry boat system was introduced to link the parks, more attention needed to be done to bring foot traffic to the new Wild Life section of the park. A pathway was installed behind Raging Wolf Bobs along the northeastern side of Geauga Lake and a floating bridge connecting the two sides of the lake was also introduced. Six Flags wanted guests to find their way to the newly acquired Sea World property. If guests were not attracted to that area of the park, it meant introducing more rides and potentially a new roller coaster. With the merger, the park was marketed as three parks for the price of one or "three worlds, one ticket" — Wild Life, Wild Rides and a waterpark — but could the new mega park service solve the company's growing debt? Attendance for the park had to grow and that was certainly a difficult task with nearby Cedar Point. Six Flags COO Gary Story envisioned the park adding a variety of new entertainment over a series of five years, as well as adding interactive, themed, and highly landscaped areas.

As the park opened for the 2001 season, park guests noticed a 40th anniversary logo. It seemed odd that a park with over 100 years of history and more by the name of Geauga Lake, rather than Six Flags, would celebrate such an anniversary. The reason for the anniversary logo was because Six Flags  was celebrating its 40th anniversary in 2001. The ambience and that deep-rooted tradition at the park seemed to all but disappeared. And while the park prided itself on delivering excitement at every corner, excitement was not what guests experienced. The park was overcrowded and became known for its poor upkeep in facility maintenance and staffing concerns. As Six Flags Incorporated purchased additional parks, the debt load of the company had a significant impact on its parks, especially Six Flags Worlds of Adventure. It was clear the park was too large to maintain and certain aspects of the operation were suffering from spending cuts. The company was headed toward bankruptcy and the possibility of closing or even selling off properties was becoming more of a reality. In late June, the park sought permission to build a 200-foot-tall roller coaster on the former Sea World property for the following year. To do so would continue the conversations of the park's corporate team trying to directly compete with Cedar Point, which at the time hosted twelve roller coasters. By July 4, 2001, it became evident the newly combined park was not successful. While the park claimed to draw close to three million visitors, many people commented on the high price of not only admission, but everything else for purchase in the park from retail, food, and game options. Although the company claimed Six Flags Worlds of Adventure saw the largest increase (up 61% to 2,750,000 guests) for 2001 out of all of the company parks, attendance was actually down 250,000 from what Six Flags Ohio and Sea World Ohio did in 2000.

Wanting to solve the dilemma of connecting the park, management did receive approval from local government officials to construct a Lost World attraction to be located in the area behind Raging Wolf Bobs. The new area was to include all sorts of exotic animals such as birds, reptiles, sharks, white tigers, kangaroos, black bears, and lemurs. What the park did not receive approval for was the 200-foot roller coaster it had planned. When these plans were cancelled, smaller park enhancements were made to the Wild Life section of the park instead. Multiple rides, mostly children rides, opened next to the Wild Life section of the park. These rides included Pirates Flight, June Bug Jump, Tea Cups, Turbo Bungy, a refurbished Yo-Yo, and the Black Squid which was relocated from the opposite side of the park. Elsewhere in the Wild Life section of the park, Tiger Island opened to the public as did Reptiles Wild. These smaller exhibits were completed to replace the Lost World attraction that would never be built. The park also secured on loan, a female orca killer whale, Shouka. The return of the killer whale show was a welcome addition to the park, especially for those who missed the shows from the Sea World days. And with the new additions came another price increase to general admission, which now sat at $40. There was hope that the addition of more animals, especially the killer whale show would help boost attendance, but the steep admission price kept guests away.

A Wild Ride Begins

With a bigger facility comes more responsibility, which in turn leads to the need for more staff. This became a major challenge for the massive operation. Staffing shortages were common at Six Flags Worlds of Adventure, and the grounds were not properly maintained to the former cleanliness standards. Maintaining the growing lineup of amusement rides and attractions was equally difficult, and the park required 30 maintenance technicians just to maintain the park's mechanical rides.

Before the 2003 season, a new traffic signal was installed on Route 43 to ease the process of exiting the park. Additionally, Geauga Lake Road was rerouted around X-Flight at the front of the park to improve vehicle traffic flow. A question prevailed; with dropping attendance, would these outside projects even be noticed or make a difference? Park management and Six Flags were optimistic. The park expanded its attractions in 2003 by unveiling a new water slide structure called Hurricane Mountain. For thrill-seeking teenagers and adults, Hurricane Mountain was the perfect opportunity to test your courage at Hurricane Harbor. Additionally, the park added the Shark Attack, which catered toward families. These new water slides were welcome additions to Hurricane Harbor, which had not seen any additions in four years. The park added two new mechanical rides, the Starfish thrill ride and Thriller Bees family ride to the growing lineup of rides in the Wild Life section. With the new ride additions, the once popular Musik Express was retired. Raging Wolf Bobs continued to receive annual maintenance work to help smooth the aging structure, and The Villain, while highly fast in speed, had already earned a reputation for being a rough ride. Standing as it had since 1925 was the Big Dipper, always reliable and operating smoothly as a trusty traditional wooden roller coaster.

For the first time in the park's history, metal detectors were added to the main gates of the park. However, something such as metal detectors did not gather the media attention as much as glaring issues found throughout the park. Many of the park's food stands were closed as were many of the rides and regardless of the reasoning, guests were not pleased. Looney Tunes and DC Super Heroes were commonly advertised as being at the park, but they were rarely found, as were live shows that were expected to occur. The continued poor appearance of the park from landscaping to general cleanliness continued to decline. Departments saw budget cuts that drastically impacted operations, guests and front-line employee satisfaction. These noticeable changes led to a drop in employees and individuals looking for summer jobs at the park.

While the Six Flags formula for success worked in other markets, that formula did not thrive in Ohio. Additionally, Kennywood, located just outside of Pittsburgh, slowly expanded their operating calendar to include a new fall and October weekend event called Phantom Fright Nights. The event was themed around Kennywood's popular Phantom's Revenge roller coaster, which was redesigned from the popular Steel Phantom without its inversions. Kennywood prided itself on a strong group sales business and a perfect blend of old-fashioned family and modern thrill rides. Even Waldameer Park in Erie, Pennsylvania started to see a shift in attendance which enabled and encouraged longtime owner Paul Nelson to develop multiple expansion plans. The market appeal for people living in northeastern Ohio shifted elsewhere and word of mouth certainly worked against Six Flags Worlds of Adventure. Six Flags even tried to downplay the park's decline in public comments and blame outside factors. Additionally, the stock price of Six Flags dropped significantly, and it was clear to investors the future of the company needed a new direction as it did not have the financial means to survive. Sadly, loyalty and appreciation to the old formula that helped make Geauga Lake into a top amusement park under the Funtime ownership was a mere memory. People's loyalty is critical for the success of any business, especially in the people driven amusement park industry. Once that loyalty is lost, it can become very difficult to earn it back. Purchasing a legacy amusement park with the attempt to turn it into a huge theme park proved to be a major error.

During the 1999-2000 offseason, the park transformed into a large construction zone. Many of the parks familiar rides were removed to make way for new themed attractions using internationally known intellectual property.

Riders had to be 48" minimum to ride The Villain, however to ride the new Batman Knight Flight, riders had to be 54".

Mike Funyak

Looney Tunes Boomtown which replaced The Wave and Rainbow Island became the parks new home for children and family friendly attraction. Unlike the older children rides in Rainbow Island, the new rides featured in Looney Tunes Boomtown allowed adults to ride with children.

Mike Funyak

As the park expanded into the property formerly known as Sea World, mechanical rides began to appear in Happy Harbor including the Scrambler now named Boardwalk Typhoon, Bounty, Black Squid, Pirates Flight, Thriller Bee, Black Widow, and Yo-Yo.

Jukebox Café

Mr. Hyde's Nasty Fall towered 131 feet over Geauga Lake, dropping brave riders in freefall from 1997 to 2005.

Shipwreck Falls provided a quick method to cool off on hot summer days. Guests who wished to not become wet during their visit could escape the heat by spending time in the Gold Nugget Arcade.

The Villain featured 12 drops with its highest being 108 feet. Known as an aggressive ride, it was also the subject of a lawsuit in its first season when a rider was injured after being hit by a foreign object or loose article. Two years later in 2002, a similar incident occurred. Loose articles are strictly prohibited on amusement rides as they pose safety hazards for guests especially if they are projected from an attraction or if they are released from a hand or fall out of a pocket.

Superman Ultimate Escape and Batman Knight Flight established the park as a serious roller coaster park. Superman Ultimate Escape was the first ride of its kind in the world while Batman Knight Flight was touted as the only floorless roller coaster in the Midwest. The ride's location and layout interacted with the lake, giving riders an additional thrill level. The ride was designed to accommodate 1600 riders per hour.

Happy Harbor

Happy Harbor net climb

Mike Funyak

CHAPTER 7

Geauga Lake Forever
2004-2007

Facing financial strain in large part due to overbearing debt, Six Flags Incorporated announced in March that Six Flags Worlds of Adventure would be sold to Cedar Fair two months prior to the opening of the 2004 operating season in a cash transaction valued at approximately $145 million. It was clear that profit margins for Six Flags Worlds of Adventure were not enough to sustain operations. Massive spending across the entire Six Flags company led to major debt that the company struggled to shake off. In the years 1999 and 2000, the company added 21 roller coasters to their parks across the chain. The purchasing of multiple parks over a period of years in the United States and Europe simply became too large to manage successfully. With every park acquisition, Six Flags restructured its debt, which over time began to heavily influence the company's business decisions.

Less than one month later, the deal was finalized, and work began to rebrand the park and remove all copyright and trademarks associated with Looney Tunes, DC Comics, and Six Flags Incorporated. The purchase agreement involved all assets of the park, including the adjacent hotel and campground, but excluded all animals currently in the Wild Life area of the park. This meant what became the Wild Life section of the park would close permanently, ending an era of live entertainment featuring animals in Northeast Ohio. Staff reductions occurred, leaving many full-time employees without jobs. In a written statement from Dick Kinzel, Cedar Fair's chairman, president and chief executive officer, said:

> "With this acquisition, we have added another successful operation to the Cedar Fair family of parks in a market we already know very well. The park offers many marketing and operational synergies and provides us with a new source of earnings and future cash flow to grow distributions for our unitholders."

Kinzel also acknowledged the park would be renamed Geauga Lake with opening day scheduled for May 1. Cedar Fair's plan was simple from the beginning: focus on the basics of operating the facility and provide a superior family experience. But before the park could open, there was a great deal of work that needed to be accomplished and the Cedar Fair team had a tough task at hand. Not only did they have to relocate, hire, and train new employees, they also had to purchase and install new signage throughout the park. Operating and training manuals and handbooks were shared from other Cedar Fair owned parks to help with the standardization of company procedures throughout each department. A new marketing strategy also had to be implemented which became tough as advertising had to be altered. Six Flags Worlds of Adventure had been advertised as "3 parks for the price of 1," but now the park was not that at all. The park was struggling with an identity crisis, and while the Geauga Lake name was a welcome change, some people never even called it Six Flags. But the name change alone wasn't the root cause of the park's identity struggles.

Cedar Fair made many difficult decisions as to what the park was going to be. One noticeable change for the 2004 season was the manner in which the midway games were operated. Gone was the showmen boardwalk-style operating method, which brought in significant revenue. Since Cedar Fair did not operate games on a commission basis, this practice was retired. Geauga Lake was the last park in the amusement industry to operate games with a commission-based system.

The Fun Is Back

The decision to focus on families and for Geauga Lake to return to being a local amusement park instead of a destination theme park was made. Many loyal guests in past years had grown to dislike the recent changes to the park. The overall family atmosphere of Geauga Lake had disappeared with the addition of high thrill roller coasters and various themed areas. The park lost its sense of community that brought people together, and Cedar Fair aimed to bring that back. The concept of rebranding the park and changing the name by Six Flags did not turn into long-term success as planned. Taking ownership of the park was not easy on many levels, but the new owners remained committed and looked forward to opening day. Bill Spehn, a 25-year veteran of Cedar Fair was promoted to vice president and general manager of Geauga Lake. Prior to moving to Geauga Lake, Spehn served as vice president of park operations at Cedar Point.

With less than one month to open the park — 21 days exactly — employees went to detailed work removing all intellectual property owned by Six Flags and/or that of Warner Brothers and DC Comics. All Batman themes were removed, including the renaming of Batman Knight Flight to Dominator and surrounding food and retail locations receiving new looks. Mind Eraser was renamed Head Spin, and Serial Thriller became Thunderhawk. Superman: Ultimate Escape became known as Steel Venom, and Road Runner Express was renamed Beaver Land Mine Ride. The once popular Looney Tunes Boom Town was simply renamed Kidworks Playzone with all of the rides receiving new names and removal of the Looney Tune characters. Hurricane Harbor waterpark was renamed Hurricane Hannah's and the popular Six Flags Fright Fest Halloween event took upon the Halloween Haunt name used at other Cedar Fair parks. Other rides retained their names and themes. Many of the park's buildings were repainted and some guests even claimed to have been able to smell fresh paint when the park opened for the season.

Shortly after taking over the park, Cedar Fair informed Six Flags' "Read to Succeed" students their tickets would not be honored at the park. Public outcry forced Cedar Fair to rescind their decision, but the tickets would only be accepted on specific operating days. Another decision that Cedar Fair made that landed in the local headlines was denying Genevieve Solinkey and her sister Viola Schryer admission to the park with their lifetime passes, which had been given to Schryer upon her retirement from the park. The passes were given to Schryer for her and her family to enjoy the park during the Funtime Inc ownership period and were honored by Premier Parks and Six Flags. While Cedar Fair did not offer lifetime passes and originally did not know what to do, management decided to let Schryer and her family into the park.

New policies were implemented at the park such as restricting riders from being permitted to leave personal items on ride platforms during the ride cycles. In the years prior, guests were permitted to do as such, and they were taken aback when this was no longer the case in 2004. Management made a note to correct this decision for the 2005 season. The park's maintenance team had their work cut out as they transitioned with new ownership. During the season, rides such as Steel Venom and Head Spin experienced brief periods of downtime and were closed to make proper corrections. Once those rides reopened, they operated well without issues. The Yo-Yo was completely refurbished, reinstalled and operated as if it was a new attraction. The Black Squid was also removed mid-season for refurbishment and reinstalled with new lightning ready for a full year in 2005. The park also relocated the secondary waterpark gate Six Flags had installed near the Bellaire Express to behind the Skyscraper.

The park earned a reputation in recent years for generic souvenirs and shirts, but under Cedar Fair, the company worked diligently to improve the retail options. New ride shirts and hats, as well as a wide range of general Geauga Lake shirts and souvenirs were now available for purchase. Even though Cedar Fair elected to close the marine park, the company admitted it underestimated the significance of the marine animals in helping to attract visitors to the park. While the park closed most of the former Wild Life side, they reopened the stadium along the lake shore by adding a ski show. Additionally, the park was earning a reputation for its rides to close for maintenance-related issues. This was something Cedar Fair aimed to quickly address and move toward operating rides at full capacity with very little downtime. Cedar Point and its parent company Cedar Fair prided themselves on safe, efficient ride maintenance and operations, and this mantra was certainly one that new General Manager Bill Spehn and company executives expected from the team at Geauga Lake. After all, not only did the company need to maintain its reputation in the industry, it needed to improve the hurting reputation of a struggling amusement park with a loyal following.

Two Park Fun

On November 10, 2004, Cedar Fair announced that a new 20-acre waterpark, Wildwater Kingdom, would be constructed on the former Sea World property. Costing more than $24 million, the new waterpark would open the first of two phases on Saturday, June 18, 2005. Admission to the new waterpark was included in the price of admission to Geauga Lake, and the new waterpark allowed for the reopening of the former wildlife gate, retail locations, restaurants, restrooms and parking facilities. The new waterpark included a new Tornado slide from manufacturer Pro Slide called Liquid Lightning. Liquid Lightning was a 60-foot-tall funnel shaped raft slide. Additionally, the new waterpark featured an action river dubbed Riptide Run, with a variety of aquatic elements including waterfalls, wave generators and interactive spray gadgets. For the families and young children, Splash Landing included a huge interactive play structure with a tipping bucket capable of emptying 1,000 gallons of water on top of guests every two minutes. A children's pool complete with waterslides, bubblers, geysers, and spray gadgets was located next to the structure, rounding out the family water activity area. A teen activity pool called Coral Cove with a water obstacle course featuring net climbs, floating cargo crossings, bubbling pools, and interactive water features was also included. Relocated from the existing waterpark was Hurricane Mountain, Ohio's tallest waterslide complex.

Other than attractions, the Pizza Pier, which opened in Wildwater Kingdom, became a popular place to sit and eat. Phase II of Wildwater Kingdom planned for 2006 included a new, 38,000-square-foot wave pool. With a new waterpark in development, the park elected to keep the Hurricane Hannah's Waterpark open in 2005 so guests could enjoy the existing wave pool, lazy river, water slides, and other family water attractions already in operation. While Hurricane Hannah's remained open for the 2005 season, the previous season marked the last for the Stingray speed slides, Neptune Falls and Hook's Lagoon, which were removed in the first few months of the year.

To help build excitement within the local community, construction photos and updates were posted to the park's website to show progress on the new Wildwater Kingdom waterpark. The new waterpark opened three weeks after its targeted opening date. This was in large part owing to the Northeastern Ohio region having one of the snowiest winters on record. One notable aspect of the new waterpark was Cedar Fair's decision to repurpose much of the existing infrastructure left over from the Sea World and Six Flags eras. Although the area had a fresh, updated look, it still carried a hint of nostalgia, preserving the traditional historic charm many guests had come to love about Geauga Lake.

When the park opened for the 2005 season, park management continued its on-going efforts to refresh the park to separate itself from the former Six Flags era. The name of the park also changed to Geauga Lake & Wildwater Kingdom in order to highlight the anticipated opening of the new waterpark. Many of the park attractions that did not see new paint in 2004 received fresh looks for 2005. Included was Thunderhawk, which not only received a new paint scheme but completely refurbished ride vehicles, allowing for a smoother rider experience. The Dodgems building also received new paint and the center island in the middle of the floor was removed. Off-season track work continued on Raging Wolf Bobs, especially around the first turn and drop. Mid-way through the season, the ride also received a much-needed second train purchased from Holiday World in Indiana, which helped cut down rider wait time. The park also installed storage shelves to seven of the ten roller coasters for

guests to leave personal belongings. While a minor detail and perhaps unnoticed, this was a welcome improvement for the ride operations team.

Over at the former Sea World or Wild Life section of the property, the maintenance team worked diligently to repaint the entire Happy Harbor net climb structure. Nearby, *Robots of Mars 4D* replaced the *Pirates 4D Adventure* in the Harbor Theater and *Dino Island II: Escape from Dino Island* replaced the *Mission: Bermuda Triangle*. The Thriller Bees reopened as did the Starfish in a new location in the parks '50s section. Rides such as the Double Loop received exit doors to prevent guests from walking up the exit path, and later in the season, new directional signage began appearing in the park, helping guests navigate the various midway pathways.

Management was determined to bring back the appeal of the park that won over so many families. With families being the priority, Peanuts characters were introduced at the park to meet and greet with guests. These ambassadors of fun were commonly found on the park midways, something that disappeared during the Six Flags era. The former Geauga Lake Shoppe was renamed Snoopy Boutique and filled with Peanuts-inspired clothing and gifts. Since the purchase of Knott's

Berry Farm in 1997, Cedar Fair acquired the intellectual rights to have the Peanuts characters and the likes of Charlie Brown, Snoopy and friends represented in their chain of parks. The opportunity to introduce these characters at Geauga Lake was an easy one, and one well received by children and families of all ages. Cedar Fair was certainly pulling out all the stops to revitalize Geauga Lake and make it a popular destination for families.

Park management also restructured admission prices and lowered them to $24.95. Early season pricing of $19.95 was put in place until the new Wildwater Kingdom opened in June. Guests saw this as another welcome change and even as a bargain. In these decisions, Cedar Fair was proving the fun was truly back at Geauga Lake. Cedar Fair reported significant growth in attendance, up 7% in July and 19% in August.

During Cedar Fair's first full year of ownership, the park saw many improvements and success in the 2005 season. Unfortunately, Geauga Lake and Wildwater Kingdom made headline news in other areas that were not so great. The park was the site of boycotts from various unions in the area because the park chose to use nonunion workers in the construction of Wildwater Kingdom. Some of those unions even chose to cancel their scheduled outings at the park. However, by mid-summer the issues were resolved. Additionally, on August 6, a hydrochloric acid spill occurred before the park opened, forcing the main entrance to be closed to visitors until the spill was contained and the area cleared. Travelers to the park had to be rerouted to enter the park via the picnic pavilions by Double Loop along Geauga Lake Road. It wasn't until the evening of that day that half of the closed-off area was reopened to guest traffic.

The 2005 season marked the 25th year of the annual Oktoberfest event. New that year was a glass-blowing demonstration and first-annual eating contest where competitors ate an abundance of German food in a timed eating match. The Lakeside Catering Pavilion was turned into a German Village area and the park featured a lot of great live entertainment. The Lakeside Catering pavilions were constructed on the former Neptune Falls and Hook's Lagoon locations returning this area of the park to Geauga Lake's early days of being a picnic area.

Ongoing Challenges

Returning the park into a popular family destination proved to be a challenge, especially with the mounting maintenance projects. After being plagued with numerous maintenance issues over the years, Mr. Hyde's Nasty Fall would fall no more. Originally placed up for sale in August 2005, the ride did not find a buyer and was removed from the park in early January 2006. The removal of the ride commonly referred to as 'Hyde's or Mr. Hyde's left a void in the park skyline that guests had become accustomed too. The ride had been problematic since it opened in 1997, and what was salvageable was sent to Cedar Point to keep Demon Drop in proper operating condition. The ferry boats, Aurora Belle and Cuyahoga Queen were placed out of service and put up for sale. The floating bridge was relocated to connect already established docks and established a more direct and convenient route to Wildwater Kingdom from the ride side. Even though the ferry boats were placed out of service, the park did introduce two 10-passenger trams to transport guests between sides via the path behind Raging Wolf Bobs as an added convenience for guests.

This area of the park became known as Power City under Cedar Fair's ownership.

As Geauga Lake prepared to open for the upcoming season, it was announced on May 22, 2006, that parent company Cedar Fair was buying Paramount Parks from CBS Corporation. Parks purchased in the $1.24 billion cash deal included Kings Island, Kings Dominion and Carowinds. This one deal essentially doubled the size of Cedar Fair in the number of parks it owned and operated with five new parks and two additional properties that the company would manage. Cedar Fair generated $569 million in revenue in calendar year 2005 compared to $423 million in generated revenue for the Paramount Parks. It was a massive deal and one that turned heads in the industry, with some questioning if the price tag was too much. Industry professionals said the same when Six Flags purchased Sea World Ohio. During a conference call with investors, Kinzel said the company would not need to "go in and rebuild them."

The Paramount Parks were indeed great parks but as Cedar Fair was still trying to revitalize Geauga Lake into a successful and profitable park, it now had to turn its attention elsewhere, which could potentially hurt the struggling Geauga Lake. The removal of Mr. Hyde's Nasty Fall left a void in the '50s midway. It did not help when the Bellaire Express monorail only operated for a brief time early in the season and never reopened. A similar situation occurred with the Skyscraper and later Steel Venom closing for maintenance in July but to not operate

again. What remained of Hurricane Hannah's waterpark was walled off and sealed from the public. With the Skyscraper and Bellaire Express now closed, the only method in seeing this once popular area of the park was by riding Shipwreck Falls or the Big Dipper.

Operating costs for the park were extremely high, and the scaling back of attractions was seen as a way to cut costs, especially given the difficulties the park had in completing necessary maintenance projects. While it was evident these projects had become prolonged, some guests speculated the Skyscraper was closed to avoid guests from seeing the former waterpark. However, with Hurricane Bay wave pool closing, it gave way for Tidal Wave Bay to open as the phase II expansion of Wildwater Kingdom. When the new wave pool opened and was met with great reviews, guests noticed that the rest of the phase two plans were cancelled. What wasn't built included speed slides, an adult pool and swim-up bar. However, 16 VIP cabanas were added to the new waterpark for guests to rent for the day. One day rentals included four chaise lounges, four inner tubes, table with umbrella, a lockable storage drawer, and food service directly to a rented cabana.

The former waterski stadium renamed as the Geauga Lake Stadium hosted live entertainment in the form of "Paul Bunyan Lumberjack Show." Over at the Palace Theater, magic shows entertained guests, and live music performers returned to the main entrance area. The park even offered a season-long promotion for Cotton Candy in which it was sold for 25 cents. While a great idea in theory, it seemed odd that such a promotion would even occur. Was the park struggling financially or did management want to simply attempt to bring attention to the importance of families and emphasize the park was affordable? This insinuated that under the Six Flags ownership, the park was known for being expensive for families. Cedar Fair was simply trying to cater to families, and they knew that many of the rides installed in recent years did not bring guests to the park. With the park having issues with ride closures again, something which Cedar Fair worked diligently to avoid, concern for the park's future began to arise. One location in which a ride formerly sat was used for a 3-Point Challenge basketball game. The former site of the Silver Bullet, still commonly referred to as the Enterprise, was no longer an eyesore, but now those feelings were directed elsewhere.

The 2006 season was cut shorter than usual when the annual Haunt event was eliminated from the operating calendar. An article in the Sandusky Register stated the reasoning for the cancellation was to prevent Geauga Lake from competing with Cedar Points Halloweekends. With Halloween being a huge moneymaker for numerous amusement parks and independent operators, many onlookers and Geauga Lake guests questioned the decision. Oktoberfest returned with its popular international cuisine on September 15-17. New for Oktoberfest in 2006 was the German Festhaus in the Gold Nugget Arcade located in the Western Village area of the park. The new food venue was themed with German-inspired décor and live entertainment, polka dancing and additional indoor dining opportunities. The park also created a German Village surrounding the Gold Nugget arcade to feature old world-trades such as glass blowing, bread making, and more. The popularity of the Wine School from the previous season was brought back in 2006 and was featured in the Palace Theater. Guests had the opportunity to sample different types of wines paired with corresponding cheeses and fruits. But Oktoberfest was always a huge event at the end of the year and now it was only three days or one weekend.

Attendance at the park rose in the latter part of the summer months. Oktoberfest was also well attended in large part due to the positive weather. But dark clouds were certainly forming over Geauga Lake, and it was not to the liking of the park staff or parent company. These fears didn't seem possible, especially not for a park that had been an entertainment destination for over 100 years. Rumors of

rides leaving the park were deemed true when it was announced in late 2006 that X-Flight would be dismantled and moved to another park within Cedar Fair, Kings Island. It was apparent now that Cedar Fair planned to downsize and "right size" the park, which was a smart business decision. The park

had a series of roller coasters that did not fit with the market in which the park catered. It was figured that thrill seekers would certainly visit Cedar Point if they were looking to ride intense and record-breaking roller coasters.

The company planned on turning Geauga Lake into a smaller regional park, similar to sister park Michigan's Adventure. A smaller park with a great lineup of attractions and loyal guests are easier to staff, operate, and maintain. After all, the company built an entirely new waterpark, so there didn't seem to be a reason for concern. Yet worries about the park's future mounted when Steel Venom was removed and sent to Dorney Park in Allentown, another sister park owned by parent company Cedar Fair. Next the Bellaire Express was removed from the park. Signs were posted at the entrances informing guests of the rides' removal. While it's never a good sign to see attractions removed from the park, it has occurred multiple times in the industry to help defray operating costs, especially when guest demand doesn't exist. It was certainly possible that Cedar Fair removed these rides for future development. The removal of those three rides did not impact Geauga Lake's attendance but for the curious guest, it still seemed strange, especially when the original park and area surrounding the Big Dipper was now quieter than ever.

There were also some noticeable changes that included *Lego Racers* replacing *Robots of Mars* and the Texas Twister receiving a new paint job. The Carriage House introduced Starbucks Coffee, and the Jukebox Café was remodeled. Some operations of the park were streamlined, especially with personnel. Cedar Point and Geauga Lake's marketing department were now one unit operating out of Cedar Point. Kennywood also ramped up its presence in the Cleveland market, launching an aggressive advertising campaign that included billboards and television spots. The group behind Kennywood and its sister parks were experienced operators with a strong reputation in the amusement industry. They too recognized the shifting market and as nostalgia for the former days of Geauga Lake grew, more and more people from the region began making the trip to parks such as Kennywood. The company helped fuel that trend by offering special online ticket options specifically targeted at Ohio travelers.

Guests wanting to visit Geauga Lake in 2007 saw a slight increase in general admission, going up two dollars from 2006, which now sat at $26.95. Junior and Senior admission were also increased two dollars to $11.95. The park also announced it would now open Saturday May 26, 2007, of Memorial Day weekend. A shortened season — even less than it was in previous seasons — was not seen as a positive sign. Parking prices were $9 per car and $14 for oversized vehicles. General season passes were $79.95, with season passes for seniors (age 62 and older) and juniors (ages 3 and older and under 48 inches) at $54. The Cedar Fair MAXX pass valid at all Cedar Fair (including the former Paramount parks) was $125.

On June 16, Raging Wolf Bobs suffered a train derailment that closed the ride for the remainder of the season. No severe injuries occurred, but now the park lost another major attraction. The Villain on the other hand had been carefully retracked over the last couple of years and saw a resurgence in popularity, especially with Raging Wolf Bobs now closed. More interestingly, less than one month later on July 9, news broke that Cedar Fair reached out to private equity firms to gauge interest in a buyout of the company on the conditions that the company's management team remain in place. One of the companies contracted to investigate the matter was Bear, Stearns & Co. Inc, which advised Cedar Fair to purchase the Paramount Parks and provided a $2 billion loan on the deal.

Shortly after the news of Cedar Fair potentially selling to a private equity firm, rumors of the possible removal of both Dominator and Thunderhawk reached the public. Further rumors pointed to the possible closure of the entire ride side of the park. When it came time for season passes to go on sale for 2008, they never became available for renewal or purchase. The park finished the year with the 27th annual Oktoberfest, and like the previous season, it was only a three-day event. The park closed for the season on September 16 and five days later on September 21, Cedar Fair shockingly announced the ride side of the park was closing permanently. Vice President and General Manager Bill Spahn, released the following statement:

> *"Beginning with the 2008 season, Geauga Lake & Wildwater Kingdom will become exclusively a waterpark attraction.*
>
> *While we know many of you enjoyed the rides and attractions of the amusement park side of the park, the waterpark has become increasingly popular over the years; Wildwater Kingdom is now our guests' favorite area. Since 2005, we have invested approximately $25 million in Wildwater Kingdom, and it has become the premier waterpark in northeastern Ohio.*
>
> *Geauga Lake has a long history and has evolved over the years since its beginning as a picnic grove. That tradition of family entertainment will continue, but in a new and exciting way."*
>
> *Geauga Lake's 2008 operating schedule, admission pricing, group programs and other operating details will be announced at a later date.*
>
> *We thank you for your past patronage and look forward to seeing you next summer at Geauga Lake's Wildwater Kingdom!"*

Soon after the announcement, it became clear Cedar Fair was not going to sell the park to another amusement park operator. As Tim O'Brien said in his autobiography on former Cedar Fair CEO Dick Kinzel, the park did not succeed under Six Flags or Cedar Fair.

Geauga Lake

Geauga Lake

Similar to the Skyscraper but 40 feet shorter, Americana provided wonderful views of park, Geauga Lake and the surrounding communities.

X-Flight

Local hotels and motels typically partnered with the park to offer package deals for overnight accommodations and admission. Purchased in the late 1990s, park owned and operated a hotel and campground. Known as the Geauga Lake Hotel and Geauga Lake Campground during the Cedar Fair era, these properties closed when the amusement rides ceased operation after the 2007 season.

Cedar Fair moved Thunder Falls from its original location next to the Skyscraper to Wildwater Kingdom for 2005. Other attractions such as the new 1,100 ft long lazy river called Riptide Run, were brand new.

Tidal Wave Bay (top photo), featured 390,000-gallons of water

Splash Landing (bottom photo) a four-story water activity structure had a tipping bucket that dropped 1,000 gallons onto guests

The Villain's turnaround

El Dorado, sat up to 40 riders in a blue 1950s style El Dorado convertible car. The ride vehicle swung riders forward and backwards as it rotated to heights of 85 feet. The ride was relocated to Kings Dominion where it operated from 2009 until 2011 when it was removed at the end of the season.

Texas Twister

Originally known as Mind Eraser and renamed Head Spin upon Cedar Fair taking ownership of the park, the ride was manufactured by Vekoma based in the Netherlands. The ride could accommodate 760 riders per hour. As seen in the photo, a platform and stairs are visible between what is called the cobra roll inversion. Should the ride vehicle stop in the middle of the cobra roll, the platform provided a method of evacuation route for riders should maintenance and management personnel need to perform such duties.

After the closure of Geauga Lake, Head Spin was relocated to Carowinds in Charlotte, North Carolina.

CHAPTER 8

The Final Years
2008-2016

With the country entering a major financial recession, a decision to close most of Geauga Lake was made. When Cedar Fair took over ownership and operations of Geauga Lake, the company implemented a three-year plan for the park. The company purchased Geauga Lake and all of its assets for $145 million. Not even 10 years prior, Six Flags purchased Sea World Ohio for $110 million. Although Cedar Point and Geauga Lake were just two hours or about 85 miles apart, the potential to expand the Cedar Fair market and brand in the region was undeniable. Cedar Fair executives understood before and after acquiring Geauga Lake, significant work would be required to keep the park operational.

Yet by 2007, it was clear the performance of the park was behind expectations, and there was no reason to believe there was an upside. In the summer of 2008, Geauga Lake & Wildwater Kingdom reopened as Geauga Lake's Wildwater Kingdom, a waterpark only. Downsizing was the only practical option for the park, and operations would need to be sustained to recoup the investments put into the facility. A wall was installed separating the former Happy Harbor area of the park that featured the amusement rides and various attractions. The floating walk bridge connecting both sides of the lake was removed and the former Geauga Lake Stadium sat idle all season. Plans to transfer and move additional assets and employee talent to other parks within the company were put into action.

The Auction

On June 17 and 18, 2008, an auction conducted by Norton Auctioneers for most rides and park-related equipment was held at the former ride side of Geauga Lake. While some watched the auction in a somber mood, most people attended the auction to capture one final glimpse of the popular amusement park. Many attendees simply came to learn the fate of the Big Dipper. There was hope the ride could be saved in its location or even be purchased by another park. Kennywood considered purchasing the roller coaster and looked at two possible locations for the ride to be installed. They reconsidered after realizing too much of its existing park would need to be redesigned and redeveloped.

The biggest challenge in finding a new home for the Big Dipper was that the coaster was designed to fit the piece of property on which it was built. Locals were certainly upset about losing a landmark, but so were other individuals such as politicians. After all, the Big Dipper was the oldest roller coaster in Ohio, and losing the coaster meant losing a piece of Ohio history, let alone one of the oldest roller coasters in the country. Remarks that the Big Dipper was being offered to the American Coaster Enthusiasts were made at the auction, but that was incorrect. Nothing was established between the park or the group known as ACE, although the members were hoping to find a new home for the ride.

During the auction, Jeff Henry, then owner of Schlitterbahn waterparks, purchased multiple rides for a proposed amusement park he planned to build in the Midwest. Equipment he purchased included Shark Attack, Turtle Beach tube slides, Kids Play Zone, Gotcha Games Foam Factory, Time Warp, Boardwalk Typhoon, Bounty, Pirates Flight, the 3D Movie Theater, and even the Aurora Belle and Cuyahoga Queen Ferry Boats. While Jeff Henry had most of the rides and

equipment he purchased at the park dismantled in a short period of time, only a portion of them were installed at the Schlitterbahn Kansas City location.

Rides such as the Thunderhawk, Dominator, Americana, and El Dorado were not included in the auction. Thunderhawk was relocated to Michigan's Adventure, Dominator moved to King's Dominion, Texas Twister went to California's Great America, Yo-Yo and Head Spin made their way south to Carowinds, and all the children's attractions in the Kidworks Playzone were relocated to Cedar Point. All these mentioned attractions opened at their new parks within the Cedar Fair chain for the 2008 operating season with the exception being Head Spin, which opened in 2009. El Dorado, Black Squid, and Americana were shipped to King's Dominion in Virginia with plans for these three rides to open in 2009, however the Black Squid was never rebuilt. Shipwreck Falls was sold prior to the auction and opened in its new location at the short-lived Celebration City in Branson, Missouri, where it was renamed Roaring Falls. While most rides found new homes in the United States, Beaver Land Mine Ride was sold and reopened overseas in 2009 at Papea Park in France.

Another ride that many people pondered about, especially during the auction, was the park's Carousel. The ride was not listed for sale and had its structure sealed off in the same manner it would've been during the typical offseason months. This could only mean one thing; the ride was safe and wouldn't be broken up similar to other carousels at past amusement park auctions. The ride was carefully dismantled after the auction and underwent a detailed restoration process by Carousel Works in Mansfield, Ohio.

In 2010, the Big Dipper was put up for auction again, this time being listed on eBay. The auction ended with no buyers, but hope for saving the ride was revived when two individuals expressed interest in purchasing the ride. That deal unfortunately collapsed, and the ride continued to sit as a reminder of the park's once storied past. The following year saw the Geauga Lake Carousel reopen at Worlds of Fun in Kansas City, Missouri. Former patrons of Geauga Lake were happy to see the ride preserved, however they were quick to notice the Geauga Lake name was quietly dropped from the name of the waterpark that remained in Ohio, now simply known as Wildwater Kingdom.

Visits to Wildwater Kingdom were somewhat unsettling, as guests saw in the distance across the lake, the parks infrastructure being reclaimed by nature. It was a sad sight to see, and the former amusement park became a safety issue with reports of people trespassing. Not only did people trespass into the former park, but they even climbed the Big Dipper's structure and were arrested. The property sat vacant and remained for sale for many years. Proposals to buy the property were submitted, but none were accepted by Cedar Fair.

End of an Era

On August 19, 2016, Cedar Fair announced Wildwater Kingdom would close for the final time on Monday, September 5. Closing the park forever on Labor Day was a fitting end to the once storied park and family entertainment facility. Each summer in the United States, Labor Day marks the end of the summer season, and for the people of Bainbridge Township and City of Aurora, it was the end of an era. At the time of the announcement, Cedar Fair determined that the time was now right to begin the transition with community leaders to develop the property for the future.

On October 16, the Big Dipper met its fate and was demolished, troubling many locals who hoped to see the ride saved. Memories of amusement rides closing in 2007 lingered, and locals were still upset that their once-popular community and family amusement park lay in ruins across the lake from Wildwater Kingdom.

The sights and sounds of Geauga Lake as an amusement park were no more. Only one attraction remained, the lake itself.

No more roller coaster rides, no more smiling faces. What remained from the amusement and waterpark would soon vanish from the grounds forever, leaving only distant memories. In 2020, the property was sold, never to be an amusement park and paving the way for future development.

On Sunday, September 17, 2017, the City of Aurora's Landmark Commission in cooperation with the Aurora Historical Society, The Geauga Lake Improvement Association, and the Ohio History Connection unveiled and dedicated the Geauga Lake Historical Marker. The double-sided marker located on the southern shore of Geauga Lake and Route 43 not only recognizes the historical significance of the former Geauga Lake Park but the Geauga Lake community. Geauga Lake as an amusement park was more than that. It was a place that rose to the top of the amusement park industry with innovative strategies, a leader in the industry. Not only was the park a haven for traditional family fun, it was also a place where people felt forever young and relived memories of years gone by. Whether from purchasing a bag of cotton candy, winning the big prize from a game or walking down the midway, Geauga Lake will be remembered as a place for special memories. When recounting Geauga Lake and its more than 100 years of existence in providing fun family entertainment, one thing will always remain, Geauga Lake was "Always a Funtime."

Mike Funyak

Appendix

1970 Brochure

1972 Brochure

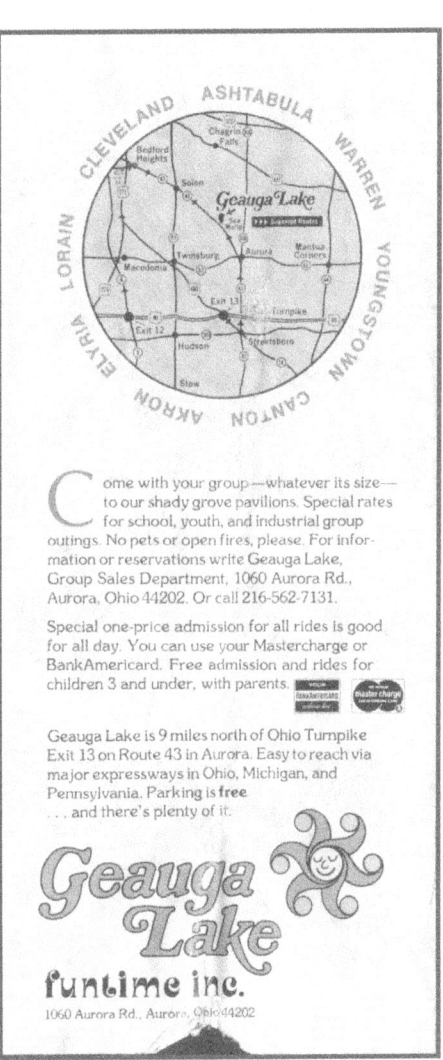

1976 Brochure

1977 Brochure

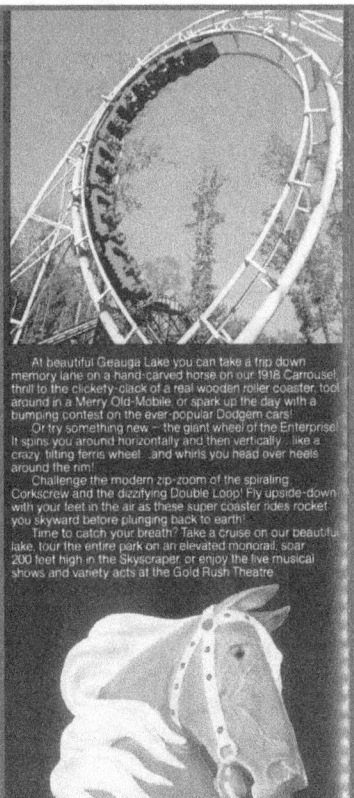

1979 Brochure

1980 Brochure

1985 Brochure

1988 Brochure

Mike Funyak

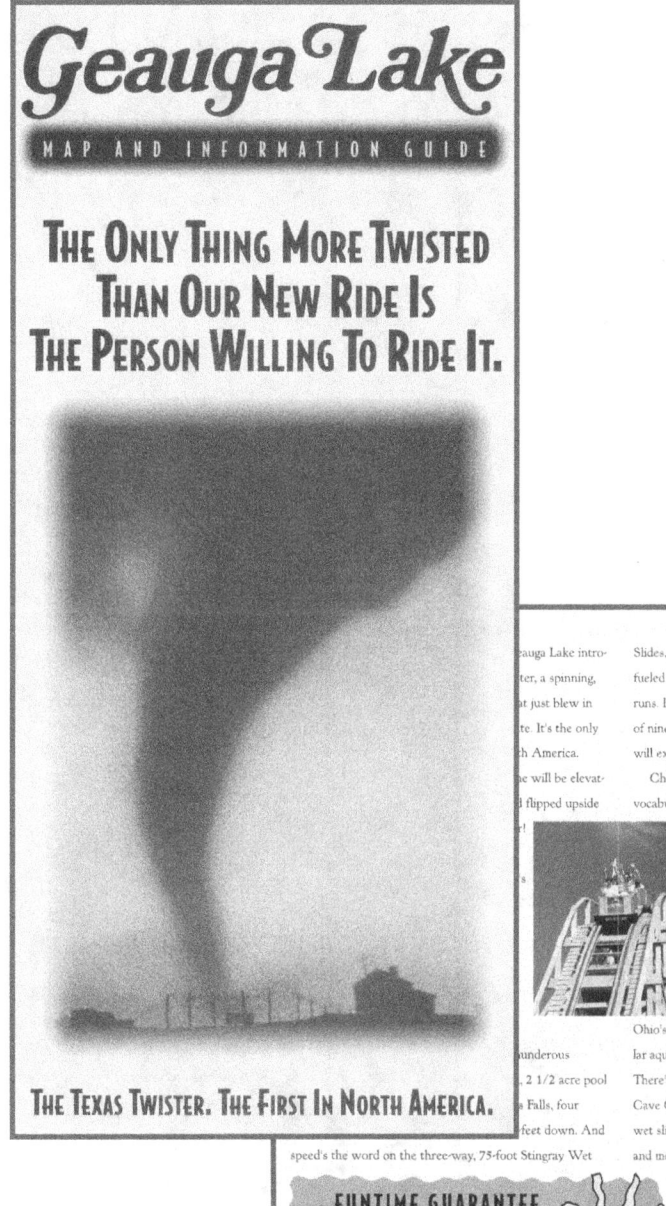

1993 Brochure

Geauga Lake

1994 Brochure

1997 Brochure

Geauga Lake

2000 Brochure

2004 Brochure

2008 Brochure

Selected Bibliography

Interviews

Bush, Lee. Email Correspondences, Phone Interviews October 27, 2024, January 22, 26, 2025

Dlugokecki, Jason. Phone and Personal Interviews, 2022-2025

Dickey, Jocko. Phone Interviews, April 25, 2025, May 2, 2025

Frato, John. Phone Interview. May 4, 2024

Henninger Jr., Harry. Phone Interviews. November 12, 2024, February 2, 2025

Samuelson Dale. Email Correspondences, Phone Interviews October 3, and 10, 2024

Shurgott, Samuel. Phone Interviews, 2022-2025

Van Voorhis, Dale. Email Correspondences, Phone and Personal Interviews, 2022-2024

Books

Francis, D. W., & Francis, D. D. (1988). Cedar Point: *The Queen of American Watering Places*. Daring Books.

Francis, D. W., & Francis, D. D. (2004). *Cleveland Amusement Park Memories: A nostalgic look back at Euclid Beach, Puritas Springs Park, Geauga Lake Park, and other Classic Parks*. Gray & Co.

Francis, D. W., & Francis, D. D. (2004). *Luna Park: Cleveland's Fairyland of Pleasure*. Amusement Park Books Inc.

Futrell, J., Hahner, D. P., & Lococo, J. (2015). *Geauga Lake: The Funtime Years 1969-1995*. Arcadia Publishing.

O'Brien, T. (2015). *Dick Kinzel: Roller coaster king of cedar point amusement park*. Casa Flamingo.

O'Brien, T. (2006). George Milay. In *Legends: Pioneers of the Amusement Park Industry* (Vol. 1, pp. 7–33). essay, Ripley Entertainment.

Smolko, T., & Taylor, J. (2014). *Geauga Lake Sunrise to Sunset*. Cleveland Landmarks Press.

Magazines

Amusement Business 1978-2001

Amusement Park Journal 1980-1987

Billboard Magazine 1921-1942, 1959

Newspapers

Cleveland Plain Dealer (Cleveland, Ohio)

Dayton Daily News (Dayton, Ohio)

The Akron Beacon Journal (Akron, Ohio)

Lancaster Eagle Gazette (Lancaster, Ohio)

The Cleveland Press (Cleveland, Ohio

The Marion Star (Marion, Ohio)

The News-Messenger (Fremont, Ohio)

The News Herald (Willoughby, Ohio)

The Times Recorder (Zanesville, Ohio)

The Pittsburgh Press (Pittsburgh, Pennsylvania)

Pittsburgh Post-Gazette (Pittsburgh, Pennsylvania)

Youngstown Vindicator (Youngstown, Ohio)

Other Sources

Amusement Park Books Collection

Aurora Historical Society

Charles and Betty Jacques Amusement Park Collection, 1873-2016. Collection 521, Eberly Special Collections Library, Pennsylvania State University, State College Pennsylvania

David and Roseann Funyak

Jason and Dawn Dlugonecki Collection

Jim Futrell Collection

Mike Funyak Collection

Dave Hahner

Gary Kyriazi

Samuel Shurgott Collection

National Amusement Park Historical Association/John Caruthers Collection

National Amusement Park Historical Association/Bowen/Hayeck Collection 1983

Photo Credits

Front and Back Cover

All photos courtesy of Charles and Betty Jacques Amusement Park Collection unless otherwise noted:

Carousel Postcard: Samuel Shurgott Collection

Guest with Geauga Dog: Samuel Shurgott Collection

Big Dipper: Samuel Shurgott Collection

Clipper train with riders: Amusement Park Books Inc.

Undertow: National Amusement Park Historical Association/Bowen/Hayeck Collection 1983

Rockets: National Amusement Park Historical Association/John Caruthers Collection

Front Matter

p. xii: Charles & Betty Jacques Amusement Park Collection (*edits by Jason Price*)

Chapter 1

All Photo and newspaper clippings from Charles and Betty Jacques Amusement Park Collection

Chapter 2

All Photos courtesy of Amusement Park Books Inc. unless otherwise noted

p. 14: Mike Funyak Collection
p. 15: Charles and Betty Jacques Amusement Park Collection
p. 37: (both photos) National Amusement Park Historical Association/John Caruthers Collection
p. 38 (top): Gary Kyriazi
p. 51 (top): Gary Kyriazi
p. 54: Charles and Betty Jacques Amusement Park Collection

Chapter 3

All Photos courtesy of Charles and Betty Jacques Amusement Park Collection unless otherwise noted

p. 63: Samuel Shurgott Collection
p. 75 (*top*): Samuel Shurgott Collection
p. 84 (*bottom*): Jason and Dawn Dlugokecki Collection

Chapter 4

All Photos courtesy of Charles and Betty Jacques Amusement Park Collection unless otherwise noted

p. 92: Samuel Shurgott Collection
p. 95: National Amusement Park Historical Association/Bowen/Hayeck Collection 1983
p. 96: National Amusement Park Historical Association/John Caruthers Collection
p. 102: Samuel Shurgott Collection
p. 104: Samuel Shurgott Collection
p. 108 (*bottom*): National Amusement Park Historical Association/Bowen/Hayeck Collection 1983

p. 110 (*bottom photos*): National Amusement Park Historical Association/Bowen/Hayeck Collection 1983

p. 111 (*top*): National Amusement Park Historical Association/Bowen/Hayeck Collection 1983

p. 111 (*bottom*) Samuel Shurgott Collection

p. 114 (*top*): Jason and Dawn Dlugokecki Collection

p. 115 (*top*): National Amusement Park Historical Association/John Caruthers Collection

p. 115 (*bottom*): National Amusement Park Historical Association/Bowen/Hayeck Collection 1983

p. 116 (*top*): Samuel Shurgott Collection

p. 116 (*bottom*) National Amusement Park Historical Association/Bowen/Hayeck Collection 1983

p. 117 (*top*): National Amusement Park Historical Association/John Caruthers Collection

p. 117 (*bottom*): Samuel Shurgott Collection

Chapter 5

All Photos courtesy of Charles and Betty Jacques Amusement Park Collection unless otherwise noted

p. 121: Jason and Dawn Dlugokecki Collection

p. 124 (*top*): Jason and Dawn Dlugokecki Collection

p. 133 (*bottom*): Jason and Dawn Dlugokecki Collection

p. 134 (*top*): David and Roseann Funyak

p. 136 (*bottom*): Samuel Shurgott Collection

p. 141 (*top*): David and Roseann Funyak

p. 146 (*top*): Jason and Dawn Dlugokecki Collection

p. 150 (*top. L*): Jason and Dawn Dlugokecki Collection

Chapter 6

All Photos courtesy of Charles and Betty Jacques Amusement Park Collection unless otherwise noted

p. 158 (*bottom*): Samuel Shurgott Collection

p. 160: Samuel Shurgott Collection

p. 161: Samuel Shurgott Collection

Chapter 7
All Photos courtesy of Charles and Betty Jacques Amusement Park Collection unless otherwise noted

p. 194 (*bottom*): Dave Hahner Collection

Chapter 8
All Photos courtesy of Charles and Betty Jacques Amusement Park Collection unless otherwise noted

p. 212 (*bottom*): Mike Funyak Collection
p. 213 (*bottom*): Mike Funyak Collection

Appendix
All park brochures courtesy of Charles and Betty Jacques Amusement Park Collection unless otherwise noted

p. 222: 1988 park brochure – Samuel Shurgott Collection
p. 223: 1993 park brochure – Samuel Shurgott Collection
p. 225: 1997 park brochure – Mike Funyak Collection
p. 227: 2004 park brochure – Samuel Shurgott Collection

About the Author

Mike Funyak, a native of Western Pennsylvania has worked in the amusement industry since 2013. He is a 2015 business school graduate from Robert Morris University in Moon Township, Pennsylvania. Following graduation and during his time working in the amusement industry, Mike has been fortunate to meet, work, and learn from multiple industry professionals and park owners.

When he is not working, Mike enjoys rooting for his hometown professional sport teams and spending time with family and friends. He is also the author of *West View Park: The Story of the T.M. Harton Company*.

www.ingramcontent.com/pod-product-compliance
Lightning Source LLC
Chambersburg PA
CBHW080747060526
44119CB00072B/168